Heroines of World War II

By the same author

The Fall of France
When Freedom Calls
Before the Storm: the Story of Bomber Command
Storm from the Skies
The Dragonflies
Strike from the Sea

Heroines of
World War II

Robert Jackson

Arthur Barker Limited
A subsidiary of Weidenfeld (Publishers) Limited

Arthur Barker Limited
11 St John's Hill, London SW11

ISBN 0 213 16566 x

Printed in Great Britain by
Bristol Typesetting Co Ltd,
Barton Manor - St Philips, Bristol

Contents

1 Atlantic Heroine

WHEN NINETEEN-YEAR-OLD 'Johnnie' Ferguson sailed from South America on the ill-fated liner *Avila Star* in July 1942, her one thought was to get to England and help the British war effort in some way. She never dreamed that ahead of her lay an ordeal that would earn her citations for gallantry – and an assured place in the annals of human endurance at sea.

On 12 June 1942, the Blue Star liner *Avila Star* sailed from Buenos Aires, outward bound across the Atlantic for Freetown, in Sierra Leone, and then for England. This was wartime, and not unnaturally many of the 194 souls on board – 28 passengers and 166 crew – were apprehensive about the voyage; but others felt that the 14,400-ton liner, with her 570-foot length pushing through the ocean at a steady 16 knots, would have more than a fighting chance of running the gauntlet of the prowling U-boats.

Nevertheless it was not reassuring to know that the submarines had already claimed the *Avila Star*'s sister ship, the *Arandora Star* – or that Lord Haw-Haw, the Nazi Propagandist, had announced over the radio that the Germans intended to sink all five A-class liners of the Blue Star Line.

However one passenger at least treated the voyage as a great adventure. Her name was Maria Elizabeth Ferguson, better known to her friends by the nickname of Johnnie. When war broke out she and her mother were in England, where Johnnie had been attending school; her father was a tea planter in the Argentine, and in June 1940 – partly because she had not seen him for a long time, and partly because her mother felt that invasion-threatened Britain was no place for the girl – she sailed for South America to join him.

The months went by and she was far from happy. Although she led a life of luxury that most seventeen-year-old girls dream about, with a seemingly endless round of swimming, sport and parties, the newsreel films of the German blitz on

Britain brought a sense of guilt that gradually turned into a deep determination to return and involve herself in the war effort.

Her eighteenth birthday came and went; her father gave his consent to her going back to Britain, although he did not want her to travel alone. For that reason she held back for several more endless months, until – in May 1942 – she learned that some friends were to make the transatlantic crossing on the *Avila Star*. She wasted no time in booking her passage, and was undeterred when, at the last moment, her friends had to cancel. She sailed with the liner on 12 June, a week before her nineteenth birthday.

On 22 June, well out into the Atlantic, the *Avila Star* stopped to pick up some survivors from the *SS Lylepark*, which had been torpedoed and sunk. More survivors from the vessel were discovered in Freetown, and some of them elected to join the *Avila Star* for the final leg of the voyage to Britain. This was the most dangerous part, for the liner's skipper, Captain John Fisher, had been warned by the Admiralty to expect intense U-boat activity between latitudes 40° and 50° north. For this reason he took the *Avila Star* northwards at full speed, following a zigzag course in the hope of eluding any shadowing submarine.

The days passed, and both passengers and crew began to relax a little. The Canary Islands and Madeira slipped past unseen, and by 5 July the liner was abeam the Azores, 150 miles away over the western horizon. At dusk the captain once more altered course and the ship proceeded under rigid blackout, nosing her way through a calm sea. The passengers had dinner and many of them went up on deck, enjoying the placid evening and watching the stars that were beginning to show through the thin veil of mist that hung over the sea to the east.

It was just after 9 o'clock when the first torpedo struck,

ripping into the *Avila Star*'s starboard side between the engine room and boiler room. The liner quickly developed a pronounced list and the captain, realizing that the position was hopeless, gave the order to abandon ship.

Johnnie Ferguson was below when the torpedo hit, between her cabin and the assistant purser's office. The lights went out and in the darkness she lost her lifejacket. Remembering her boat drill, she groped her way on deck and headed through the confusion to her station at no. 7 lifeboat, on the liner's starboard side. Together with several others she scrambled aboard, and a few seconds later the boat was floating safely on the swell. The other lifeboats were already pulling away from the stricken ship; the crew of no. 7 stood by to pick up survivors who were floundering in the sea close to the liner's hull.

At that moment the second torpedo struck, exploding against the ship's side 15 feet under no. 7 lifeboat. The blast blew the boat completely out of the water and flung its crew through the air in all directions. Something struck Johnnie on the head and then, in a daze, she was struggling in the sea. The shock of the water cleared her head a little, and as she surfaced she saw that the shattered no. 7 boat was still afloat, prevented from sinking by its buoyancy tanks. Choking in the fuel oil that covered her from head to foot, she struck out towards it; someone hauled her aboard and she lay gasping in its sodden stern.

Some time later, when she had recovered a little, she sat up and looked round. It was a nightmarish scene; the great hull of the liner, terrifyingly close and getting lower in the water with every passing minute, was surrounded by a sea of debris and oil in which the lifeboats drifted, searching for survivors whose cries could be heard. She helped to drag a couple of injured men into her own boat and tried to comfort them as best she could – then, in horror, saw the purser,

Weston, vanish under the surface before anyone could get to him.

The main thing now was to get away from the *Avila Star* before she slid to her grave and dragged them down with her. Desperately, the oil-drenched survivors in the seven boats pulled away from the stricken ship; they were so intent on their task that few saw her go down. One instant she was there, the next she was gone, and they were alone on the limitless ocean – with an enemy submarine close at hand.

All of them had heard stories about German U-boat captains machine-gunning helpless survivors. This man, however, was of a different calibre. Not only had he delayed firing his second torpedo for thirty minutes, to enable the boats to get clear, but later – as the survivors eventually learned – he surfaced at considerable risk to his ship and crew to pass on the position of the sinking to the crew of a neutral Portuguese destroyer.

The lifeboats managed to cling together in the darkness, flashing signal torches to maintain contact. It was bitterly cold, and Johnnie – suffering now from the delayed effects of shock – was repeatedly sick because of the oil she had swallowed. Nevertheless she did what she could to nurse the four injured men in boat no. 7; two had broken bones, a third was in deep shock and the fourth, horribly scalded over much of his body, was in continual intense agony. To add to their problems, although the lifeboat was still floating it was constantly awash, which made it impossible to get the injured men out of the water.

The hours of darkness dragged by endlessly. With the coming of dawn, it was found that boat no. 1 was missing. Now, for the first time, the rest saw each other clearly; the oil-spattered, red-eyed faces of the dozen people in Johnnie's boat swam into focus, and looking round she saw that some of the other boats were desperately overloaded. As soon as it

was daylight the survivors were distributed more evenly
among the little craft. The injured men from boat no. 7 were
transferred to no. 4, while the remainder – including Johnnie –
went across to no. 2. Soon afterwards, the battered lifeboat
no. 7 sank. During the morning the survivors' flagging spirits
received a boost when the stray no. 1 boat was sighted; it
eventually joined up with them.

There were 38 souls on board no. 2 boat, under the command of the *Avila Star*'s second and third officers, John Anson
and Richard Clarke. In all 160 people had survived the disaster.

When all the survivors had been accounted for the chief
officer, Eric Pearce – in no. 4 boat – gave the order for the
tiny convoy to steer east-north-east, towards the coast of
Portugal, between 500 and 600 miles away. Even if they
drifted south and missed Portugal, Pearce reasoned, they
would make landfall somewhere on the long coastline of north-
western Africa. Under favourable conditions the voyage
should take about ten days, which meant that rationing had
to be strict. Water was the most vital commodity of all, and
this was allocated on the basis of $4\frac{1}{2}$ ounces per person per day.

Throughout the first day, Johnnie – together with another
female survivor, Pat Traunter, with whom she had shared
a cabin on the ill-fated liner – busied herself with attending
to the needs of the injured. The worst case in boat no. 2 was
McIndoe, the assistant larder cook, who had a badly smashed
hand and wrist; then came Kelly, the steward, with a severely
split left eyebrow.

During the night of 6-7 July the boats inevitably began to
split up, and by noon on the seventh only two – nos. 2 and 6 –
were still in company. By this time the injured – the effects
of shock having begun to wear off – were suffering intense
pain, and another survivor in no. 2 was seized by a severe
attack of dysentery. Others, too, began to show signs of sick-

ness, and the sanitary problem became a real worry. Johnnie was fortunate in that her head injury gave her no trouble; her own earlier sickness had now disappeared, and after she had cleaned the oil from her skin with the aid of a little petrol she began to feel much better.

The two boats drifted on during 8 July, their passengers wondering how the other boats were faring – and never dreaming that the 110 survivors aboard them were at that moment being picked up by a Portuguese destroyer, the *Lima*. The warship immediately embarked on a search for boats 2 and 6, but it revealed nothing and the Portuguese captain resumed his course for the Azores.

On 10 July the crews of boats 2 and 6 – which had somehow managed to stay together – reckoned that they were now about 400 miles off the coast of Portugal. What they did not know, however, was that the tide was gradually taking them further south. The wind was now blowing from the north-north-east and freshening steadily accompanied by a growing swell and occasional rain squalls. During the afternoon the wind strength increased, whipping up the sea into broken crests that burst in freezing spray over the tossing boats and their occupants. That night was fearful. The boats streamed their sea anchors and their crews huddled together, shivering and soaked through, in the hope that the adverse weather would pass by morning. If anything, however, the weather grew even worse with the coming of dawn; although the sky cleared somewhat, 10-foot waves tossed the lifeboats like corks from one trough to the next. Almost everyone was seasick; even Johnnie, who had managed to remain cheerful during the long hours of darkness to give encouragement to the injured men, was now overcome by despair as one great wave after another flung sheets of water over her.

That night the two boats once again streamed their sea anchors. At daybreak on 12 July – the seventh dawn – the occupants of boat no. 2 searched the sea for their companion craft, but it had gone. Lifeboat no. 6 was never seen again.

Boat no. 2, alone now, sailed on, its occupants saddened by the loss. They were all badly frightened, and thinking seriously about death for the first time since the sinking. When she was not helping to tend the sick Johnnie sat as though hypnotized, watching the great waves that towered over the boat and wondering, as each one crashed down in a burst of foam, whether this would be the one that finally sank them.

It was only a question of time before someone broke under the strain. It happened on 13 July, when – after another night of cold, sickness and misery – a passenger named Ferreyra became delirious and jumped overboard, shouting that he was going for a bathe. The boat's crew searched for him for fifty minutes, until they were exhausted, but the waves had swallowed him for ever. The tragedy numbed them all; there was very little talking in the boat during the remainder of that day. The night of 13-14 July was the worst yet, with the boat plunging head-on into massive waves that rose higher than the mast. Everyone who was fit enough to do so baled out furiously with anything to hand as the water came flooding in. They were all utterly exhausted by daybreak, and the condition of the sick had taken a marked turn for the worse during the hours of darkness. McIndoe, in particular, was in great pain; his injured foot was swollen and angry-looking, and Johnnie suspected that gangrene was developing.

It was over a week now since the sinking, and even the uninjured in no. 2 lifeboat were wondering how much longer they could survive. The food situation was fast becoming critical; during the first week the meagre ration of food and water had been just enough to sustain them, but now the water had become brackish and foul-tasting and thirsts were growing desperate.

Many of the boat's occupants were by this time too dehy-

drated and weak to chew what little food was issued. Hard-
tack biscuits were soaked in sea water to soften them, but this
made the eater even thirstier. Johnnie's time was now taken
up with nursing another sick passenger, Mr Florence, who
was suffering from dysentery and exposure. By the afternoon
of the seventeenth he was delirious, and shortly before dusk
he died in the girl's arms. They said a few prayers, then gently
laid his body over the side. By 20 July, with two cans of the
precious water gone and the third – and last – under strict
ration, thirst was an ever present horror. One of the crew
went out of his mind and gulped seawater; he died later that
day. Three more men followed him on the twenty-first.

To Johnnie, everyone in the boat looked like a living
skeleton; it never occurred to her that she must look the same.
As time went by she found it increasingly difficult to dis-
tinguish between the living and the dead; they were all weak
and listless now, lying motionless with their own private tor-
ments. She was unaware that to most of them she had become
a symbol of courage; they looked at her as she sat in the stern
or moved among the sick and drew strength from her quiet
fortitude.

Another crew member died during the night of 21-2 July;
the next morning his body was put quietly over the side in a
ritual that had become all too familiar. The rest lay there,
tongues swollen in parched mouths that seemed filled with
cotton-wool, and wondered whose turn it would be next. The
hours of the morning dragged on, the sun now beating down
mercilessly from a cloudless sky. Suddenly, at 11 o'clock, they
heard it: the faraway drone of aero engines. A wave of
feverish excitement swept through the boat. Fear too – in case
the aircraft flew away without sighting the tiny speck drifting
in the middle of the ocean. With trembling hands the boat's
crew sent up a couple of flares, and prayed as they had never
prayed before. Men wept as the tension grew unbearable.

Then, miraculously, the drone of the engines began to grow louder.

A few moments later, a croaking cheer went up as two aircraft came into sight, flying low out of the west. Despite her weakness Johnnie stood upright and waved furiously – then froze, together with the rest of the boat's occupants, as she saw that the aircraft carried crosses on their fuselage sides. For a split second, she had the wild fear that they had come all this way and endured so many hardships only to be machine-gunned by German aircraft.

But the crosses were the red and yellow markings of neutral Portugal, not the black insignia of Nazi Germany. The aircraft circled the boat, then made a run-in and dropped a couple of canisters, which were retrieved by two crew members who made a supreme effort and dived overboard for them. The first canister contained water, which was shared out at once; the second carried a chart, with their approximate position marked on it and the scrawled message: 'Good luck and courage. Help will come soon. Portuguese Naval Aviation.'

The chart told them that they were a long way off their intended track; in fact they had been drifting steadily east-south-east all the time, and were still 200 miles from land. Nevertheless, now that they had been sighted they all felt that it was only a question of hours before a surface vessel came up to rescue them; for the first time since they had become separated from the unfortunate no. 6 boat, hopes once more began to run high. So they steeled themselves to endure their nineteenth night at sea, confident that the next day – Thursday, 23 July – would see the end of their ordeal.

Later those that survived were to remember it as Black Thursday. It began, not long after dawn, with the death of Donald McIndoe, the larder cook with the injured foot whom

Johnnie had nursed so faithfully all along. It was tragic that he should die now, with help just over the horizon. He was the eighth. . . .

The day wore on, and there was no sign of the desperately awaited ship. They scanned the horizon with burning, salt-rimed eyes, but there was nothing except the molten ball of the sun and the endless ocean. They seemed doomed to drift on helplessly, dying one by one, their agony growing sharper with the passing of the hours. Night came again, but no one slept. A haze lay across the surface of the sea, and to their torment was added the fear that the morning would find them shrouded in fog – with all hope of rescue gone for ever.

Daybreak came; the sky remained clear and for that they were grateful, but there was a grim reminder of the fate that confronted them when, at eight o'clock, the ninth man died. For the rest of them, time ceased to have any meaning. They were at a low ebb now, and by the time night fell once more even the optimistic Johnnie had almost given up hope.

It was at 10 o'clock the next morning – 25 July – that a keen-eyed look-out sighted a mast on the horizon. Wild elation seized them; they sent up flares and set light to anything that would make smoke.

A few minutes later they knew with certainty that the ship had sighted them and was coming towards them. She was the Portuguese sloop *Pedro Nunes*, and her captain's log makes brief mention of the incident which, to the last survivors of the *Avila Star*, was like being born all over again : 'At 1130 hours the Pedro Nunes sighted a lifeboat at 33°14′N, 10°3′W. Towards 1200 hours the rescue of the survivors commenced. There were twenty-eight in all; one of them – the steward Clarke – arrived dead at the ship's sick bay. At 1240, the NRP Pedro Nunes headed for Lisbon.' Tragically, Clarke was not the last to die. Three more men were also too far gone for recovery, and although the ship's doctors fought tenaciously to save their lives they died not long after the *Pedro Nunes* reached harbour.

Johnnie Ferguson remembered little of the voyage to Lisbon. She spent most of it fast asleep, waking only to take long, luxurious drinks from a carafe of water that she kept by her bunk.

The sloop reached harbour on Sunday, 26 July, and the survivors were immediately transferred to hospital. Johnnie, who shared a room with the other female survivor, Pat Traunter, had emerged from her ordeal with surprisingly little physical damage; apart from the effects of malnutrition and dehydration, her greatest discomfort was caused by seawater boils. She had no fewer than forty-eight of them, all as big as carbuncles, scattered over her body from head to foot. They were extremely painful when they came into contact with anything, and they took a long time to heal.

By 9 August Johnnie and Pat were sufficiently recovered to be moved from the hospital to the home of a British couple in Lisbon. Four days later, the two girls boarded a transport aircraft bound for Britain. Ahead of them lay six months of convalescence while their bodies readjusted to normality.

In November 1942 twenty-four people who had survived the *Avila Star* disaster were decorated for bravery. Johnnie Ferguson received the British Empire Medal. The citation read: 'One of the passengers, Miss Ferguson, showed great courage. She sat in the stern of a waterlogged boat throughout the night nursing four injured men. When the Second Officer's boat came up at daylight, she dived over the side and swam to it. She was covered with oil fuel but made no fuss about that, and her general behaviour during the twenty days' ordeal that followed was magnificent. . . .'

Later she also became the first ever woman passenger to be awarded the coveted Lloyd's Medal for bravery at sea.

It might have been thought that Johnnie, after three weeks adrift in a lifeboat, would have had enough of the sea and ships. But she was still determined to 'do her bit', and on her recovery she applied to join the WRNS – in the trade of boat's crew.

She was summoned for an interview at a WRNS recruiting office in London, where a woman officer filled in the appropriate forms. At one stage she asked Johnnie whether she had any boating experience. 'Yes,' the girl answered simply.

2 Russia's Death or Glory Girl

THE RUSSIAN PEOPLE'S struggle against the German invader between 1941 and 1945 was characterized by a fanatical kind of courage that led to countless sacrifices. This is the story of one girl's part in that struggle; a girl whose quiet charm and selflessness made her a legend.

On 22 June 1941, following his series of victories in the Balkans, Hitler launched 'Operation Barbarossa', the invasion of the Soviet Union. Along a 1,000-mile front 120 German divisions, supported by a massive concentration of artillery, armour and air power, launched themselves into Russian territory. The armoured divisions, using the classic tactics developed during the Battle of France a year earlier, speared towards their initial objectives in clouds of yellow dust, while dive-bombers shattered enemy resistance in their path.

For the Russian armies, the first weeks of the German offensive were catastrophic. Everywhere the Luftwaffe was mistress of the sky and the German armoured columns swept the crumbling Russian defences aside as they raced on to capture one Russian town after another. Minsk, Smolensk, Kiev, Novgorod – all fell under the German hammer before the autumn rains churned the dusty earth to mud and the offensive began to lose its impetus.

As the first snows of the freezing Russian winter descended on the steppes the Germans reached the gates of Moscow itself; and there they halted, as they did along the entire front, isolated in a frozen wilderness, trapped in the grip of the worst winter that Russia had known in living memory.

For the Russians, that winter meant survival. It bought them time, enabling them to build fresh armies in the east – armies that, with the approach of spring, might stem the German flood tide for long enough for Russia to draw on her almost limitless reserves of manpower and train them for the great battles that were to come.

In Moscow the thunder of guns could be heard daily, rumbling over the western horizon. The capital was well within range of the Luftwaffe's medium bombers, too, and night after night the Heinkels and Dorniers droned overhead, braving the most intense concentration of anti-aircraft fire in the history of modern warfare to pound the factories and marshalling yards that lay round Moscow's perimeter. Every day the citizens of Moscow scanned the ever-growing casualty lists in *Pravda*; there was always a husband, a brother, a son among the fallen.

Now, in November, the fog and the snow brought with them some measure of relief. The raids by the Luftwaffe became fewer, the rumble of gunfire in the west more muted. For the first time since June the Russians began to show optimism; there was a feeling that time was on their side. Out of the depths of winter their new armies would strike, and then it would be the turn of the Wehrmacht to know the bitter taste of defeat.

One morning late in November a girl walked down the steps of Moscow State University. In the street she paused and looked back with a sense of sorrow, conscious that she might never pass through its great doors again. Her name was Eugenie Rudneva and she was a slim twenty-year-old with fair hair and laughing blue eyes that endeared her to all who knew her. Just a few days earlier Eugenie had been wondering how she, too, could help in the fight against the German invaders. She had been on the point of volunteering to work in a factory when, in one of the Russian newspapers, she had read an article that told of the formation of a new Women's Air Corps. It was commanded by a woman pilot named Major Marina Reskova, who before the war had helped to pioneer several new air routes while flying for Aeroflot, the Soviet airline.

At first Eugenie had thought that the primary task of the

Women's Air Corps would be to ferry aircraft from the factory
to the various Russian squadrons, but when she found out
more about it she learned that this was far from the case. The
Women's Air Corps was to be a fully fledged combat unit, its
members flying fighters and bombers as an integral part of the
Soviet Air Force. Although most of its crews would be drawn
from the substantial ranks of qualified Soviet women pilots,
there were openings for navigators and observers.

Eugenie, who had a thorough grounding in mathematics
and geography, felt that she could easily qualify for the post
of navigator, and lost no time in volunteering. She was quickly
selected and posted to an initial training-school near Moscow,
where she found herself in the company of female volunteers
from all over Russia – members of flying clubs and gliding
clubs or, like herself, straight from school, all of them rubbing
shoulders with seasoned women pilots with thousands of hours'
flying behind them.

Eugenie and her colleagues soon found that the flying school
in no way differed from any other Soviet air force training
establishment. In addition to their basic training of drill and
ground-school subjects such as navigation and airmanship,
which most of them enjoyed, they were also subjected to a
considerable amount of political indoctrination, which most
of them did not. For Eugenie, the highlight of the course came
when she was taken for a short air experience flight in an
elderly PO-2 biplane. Although it was bitterly cold in the open
cockpit she enjoyed every minute of it – little dreaming that
it was in this very type of aircraft that she was later to rise to
fame.

The initial course ended in December 1941 with a passing-
out parade. Afterwards the girls crowded round the notice
board to see where they had been posted, and Eugenie was
delighted to find that she was to join a bomber unit based on
an airfield close to the banks of the River Volga.

If Eugenie had thought that she had learned a lot during the initial course near Moscow, however, she was soon to be proved wrong. As soon as she arrived at the new airfield she was thrown straight into a ninety-day course of advanced training designed to make her fully proficient in her new task. She plunged enthusiastically into the long, arduous ground-school sessions, gradually acquiring a thorough knowledge of aerodynamics and air navigation. Some of the other girls on the course collapsed under the strain, falling by the wayside and being transferred to non-operational duties. Everyone was sympathetic towards these failures, for no one truly believed that it was possible to turn these young, inexperienced girls into proficient airwomen in the space of a few weeks. The best that could be done with them was to try to assess their aptitude for carrying out what was essentially a difficult and dangerous task.

As time went by Eugenie was able to put her new-found knowledge to practical use in the air. Throughout the course she had been a star pupil, and her superiors soon found that their faith in her had been entirely justified. She came out with top marks in all the navigation examinations, and before long she qualified for the award of the Soviet Air Force navigator's badge – a bomb, superimposed on wings, worn on the left sleeve.

Meanwhile, as winter gave way to the spring of 1942, the war continued to go badly for the Russians. The German advance had been held on the Moscow front, but in the south the German armies were pushing on towards the Crimea – and beyond it the vital oilfields of the Caucasus – while in the north the city of Leningrad, which had become the very symbol of Russian resistance, was almost surrounded by a ring of fire and steel.

In May 1942 Eugenie was posted to the 588th Night Bomber Regiment, which formed part of the Soviet Air

Force's 122nd Air Division. The 588th was staffed entirely by women aircrews and was under the command of a veteran woman pilot named Captain Eudocie Bershanskaya. The unit was fully operational, flying from a series of airfields on the southern front in the valley of the Don. It was equipped with little PO-2 biplanes, the same type as the one in which Eugenie had been taken on her first flight. A flight of these tiny aircraft was attached to most bomber regiments; they would act as pathfinders, crossing the enemy lines under cover of darkness and dropping flares on targets in enemy territory, lighting the way for the bombers that followed. The PO-2s, fitted with a machine-gun in the rear cockpit, were also used to strafe enemy flak batteries and searchlights, as well as carrying out small 'nuisance raids' in ones and twos, carrying fragmentation bombs which the navigator dropped over the side. The German propaganda machine made light of the PO-2s, referring to them contemptuously as 'Russian plywood' or 'coffee grinders', but accounts of the fighting on the eastern front written by German soldiers since the war have revealed that these nuisance raids had a considerable psychological effect, keeping combat-weary troops in a state of nervous tension during the hours of darkness. The Germans were unable to detect the presence of the PO-2s until the first bombs came whistling down, for the Russian pilots would cross the lines at maximum height and then switch off their engines, gliding down soundlessly towards their targets. The little machines had a top speed of only 96 miles per hour and their two crew members were fully exposed to the weather in the open cockpits.

Eugenie's first pilot was a twenty-three-year-old lieutenant named Nina Raspopova. Night after night, the two girls took off from their grass airstrip near the Don and ranged over the enemy lines in the Crimea, unloading their small bombs on whatever targets they could find. To increase the number of bombs they could carry, they had the defensive machine-gun removed from their aircraft. This meant that if they were attacked by an enemy fighter, they had no means of defending themselves. Apart from the bombs, their only weapons were an army revolver and a signal pistol that fired recognition cartridges.

For the two girls the most hectic time came in the summer, when the Germans launched a new offensive. They carried out several sorties in the course of a single night, flying in all kinds of weather. Often when the ground was obscured by fog and cloud, it was only Eugenie's skill that brought them back to base; other less proficient navigators were lost with their aircraft.

By September 1942 Eugenie had become so proficient at air navigation that she was promoted to the position of regimental air navigator, and her name began to appear frequently in the Red Army's daily news bulletins. Her growing fame did nothing to weaken the bonds of close friendship she had forged with the eighty other pilots and navigators of the 588th Air Regiment; they called her ' Shenia the theorist ', because whenever she was not flying she could be found in her quarters, poring over navigation textbooks or lecturing the other girls on navigational theory. Time and again she hammered home the lesson that navigators had to make themselves as highly skilled as possible, not only for their sake but for the sake of their pilots. In the course of one lecture she told her colleagues : ' The pilot is the captain of the aircraft. If she is killed the aircraft cannot keep in the air. But great responsibility and courage is demanded of the navigator; her job is to direct the aircraft to the right position, and she suffers with the pilot for all the pilot's mistakes.'.

For Eugenie and the other women of the 588th Air Regiment the period of maximum effort came towards the end of 1942, when the unit was transferred to the Stalingrad and

North Caucasus fronts to take part in the great battle that
would end in 1943 with the destruction of the German Sixth
Army in the Stalingrad Pocket. During this period each aircraft flew up to six missions a night, the female crews dropping
over 50,000 pounds of bombs in the course of 194 raids and
totalling 216 hours' flying time.

It was during the battle for Stalingrad that another women's
air unit made its operational debut. This was the 586th Fighter
Air Regiment; equipped with Yak-7 fighters it began to dis-
tinguish itself almost immediately. One of the 586th's pilots,
Olga Yamshchikova, became the first woman fighter pilot to
destroy an enemy aircraft at night, shooting down a Junkers-
88 over Stalingrad on 24 September 1942. During the remainder of the war the 586th remained a first-line unit, supporting the Soviet armies in their subsequent advance across
Europe.

The 588th, meanwhile, soldiered on with its ancient PO-2s,
and despite their outdated equipment its crews often scored
spectacular successes. On one occasion, while attacking targets
in the Mozdok area, Eugenie bombed and destroyed the headquarters of the German Panzer leader, Field Marshal Ewald
von Kleist, an exploit that earned her high praise from the
commander-in-chief of the North Caucasus front, General
Petrov.

By the middle of 1943 the Germans were on the defensive
everywhere, and making determined efforts to consolidate
the ground they still held. One immediate result of this defensive policy was that the German anti-aircraft defences became
stiffer than ever before, and the women of the 588th Air
Regiment began to run into tremendous concentrations of
enemy anti-aircraft fire during their nightly excursions across
the front line. One of the most disastrous nights for the regiment came in 1 August 1943, when six PO-2s took off to
carry out a bombing attack on Kievskaya. As she approached

the target Eugenie, on this occasion flying with Claudia Serebryakova, who had once been an instructor with the Tbilisi Aero Club, suddenly saw the sky ahead lit up with a blaze of anti-aircraft fire and searchlights. As she watched a tiny silver cross appeared, trapped like a moth in one of the searchlight beams. It was the PO-2 piloted by Eugenie Krutova, the regiment's senior pilot. A moment later there was a flicker of flame and the aircraft plunged earthwards like a fiery comet, its bombs still on board, to explode among the German positions.

Within minutes three more PO-2s had also been shot down, exploding in mid-air as anti-aircraft shells found their cargo of bombs. Eight of the regiment's airwomen were killed that night.

It was the first time that Eugenie had actually seen any of her comrades die in combat, and the incident made a deep impression on her. Although now a veteran airwoman with hundreds of operational flights behind her, she was still only twenty-two years old; and now, for the first time, she began to think seriously about the possibility that she, too, might soon have to die in a blazing aircraft. 'If it must happen,' she wrote in her diary, 'let it be quick and easy. I do not want to die by fire, nor do I want to be taken prisoner by the enemy. If I am ever hit and catch fire, I shall order my pilot to hurl the aircraft at the Nazis. We have agreed that this is what we should do. They will never burn me.'

She was not alone in these thoughts; already several Russian airmen had chosen to die by diving their crippled aircraft on to the enemy rather than bale out and be captured. The first to do so had been a bomber pilot, Captain N.F. Gastello, who in June 1941 – at the time of the first German offensive – had deliberately crashed his bomb-laden aircraft on to a German armoured column. Other Russian pilots had been known to sacrifice their lives by ramming enemy bombers rather than break off the fight after running out of ammunition.

Soon afterwards, however, something happened that helped to dispel such gloomy thoughts from Eugenie's mind, at least for a time. Early in the New Year of 1944 she was awarded the title 'Hero of the Soviet Union', Russia's top decoration for gallantry. She was the first woman navigator in the Soviet Air Force to receive the much-coveted gold star.

In February, for the first time since she became an operational flier, she left the front and flew home to Moscow to enjoy a well-earned spell of leave. The city was lifeless and drab, the inhabitants were pale and thin as they stood silently in the long food queues or went about their unsmiling business. There was drabness everywhere; drab uniforms of army, navy and air force personnel, drab faces of soldiers who had seen too many horrors and who would soon have to return to the front to face many more.

Yet in the midst of all the greyness and despondency, Eugenie found a flash of sunshine. It came in the person of a Captain Ivan Slavik, an officer in a guards armoured regiment. The two fell in love and within days they were engaged. Then all too soon Eugenie had to return to the front.

On the wall of her quarters there hung a calendar. On it Eugenie had ticked off the number of missions she had flown. To date the total stood at 644; half-jokingly, she told her friends that when the total reached 700 the war would be over and she would be free to go home and marry her Slavik.

On 9 April 1944 Guards Lieutenant Eugenie Rudneva, regimental navigator, took off on her 645th mission, a bombing attack on a German airfield at Bulganak. On this occasion her pilot was a young and relatively inexperienced girl named Prokofyeva. They were followed by three more PO-2s, all bound for the same objective. As they approached the target they flew into a storm of anti-aircraft fire and a blinding glare of searchlights. The crews of the three aircraft that came behind saw Eugenie's machine caught and held by one of the wavering beams. Within seconds it was enmeshed in a spider's web of twinkling red flak bursts.

There was a flash, and the little aircraft began to burn. Then its nose went down and it plummeted in a headlong dive towards the enemy installations, trailing a long ribbon of flame in its wake. Eugenie was keeping her vow : she would not let them burn her. Horrified, the other airwomen watched the aircraft's final plunge. As it fell, a cascade of multi-coloured signal flares burst from it. Eugenie was saying goodbye.

There was a brief burst of flame on the ground, an explosion, and then the darkness closed in again. Sick at heart, the other crews dropped their bombs and turned for home.

A week later the Red Army occupied Bulganak. On the orders of the commander-in-chief himself, troops combed the area thoroughly for a trace of the crashed aircraft and its two occupants. But the bodies of Prokofyeva and Eugenie Rudneva, Hero of the Soviet Union, were never found.

3 Hannah Senesh: Martyr for her Cause

IT TOOK a special kind of courage for a young Jewish girl to be parachuted into the heart of Nazi-occupied Europe – with the sure knowledge that torture and death would be her lot if she were captured. Yet Hannah Senesh took the risk – for she was a crusader with a mission. Millions of her people were being murdered, and she felt it her sacred duty to try to save at least some of them.

B

On the night of 14 March 1944 a four-engined Halifax bomber lifted away from the allied airfield at Brindisi, in Italy, and set course into the northern darkness. From the outside this aircraft appeared no different from its hundreds of counterparts that, together with the Lancasters of RAF Bomber Command, were battering the Third Reich into submission night after night; but there the similarity ended.

This Halifax carried no bombs. Instead, cut into the metal floor of the fuselage, was a circular hatch, and inside the fuselage hard metal benches were riveted to the sides. The aircraft, in fact, belonged to one of the RAF's most secret units – No. 138 (Special Duties) Squadron. Night after night, flown mainly by Polish aircrews, the squadron's aircraft flew solitary missions deep into the heart of enemy territory, dropping agents, saboteurs and supplies to the various resistance groups.

On this March night in 1944 the four people who crouched inside the Halifax's vibrating fuselage all had one thing in common: they were all Jewish. There was Reuven Dafne, who had been an officer in the British Army; Abba Berdichev and Yonah Rosen, both of whom had worked on a kibbutz in Palestine before volunteering for parachute training; and finally Hannah Senesh, an attractive twenty-four-year-old girl whose presence had caused the Polish bomber crew to raise their eyebrows earlier that night.

The road that had led Hannah Senesh to her place in the frigid interior of a British bomber in the sky over war-torn Europe had been long and arduous. It began in Budapest in

1921, the year of her birth. Her father, Bela Senesh, a writer, had been highly respected not only among the Jewish community of the Hungarian capital but in literary circles throughout the country. Apart from being a successful playwright, he had contributed a weekly satirical column to the Sunday supplement of one of Hungary's leading newspapers.

In fact the Senesh family – consisting of Bela, his wife Catherine, daughter Hannah and son George – were fortunate in that Hungary, in the years following World War One, had been one of the least anti-Jewish of all European nations. There were over a million Jews in the country, many of them members of the nobility and holding senior government positions. Large numbers, assimilating themselves completely into the pattern of their adopted homeland, had become Christians, adopting Hungarian names and customs. If there had been discrimination at all it was against the relatively few Orthodox Jews, who isolated themselves almost completely from the rest of the community and were distrusted as a consequence.

It was in 1920 that the situation had begun to alter for the worse. The government of the day, led by Bela Kun, had been toppled and replaced by a virtual dictatorship under Admiral Miklos Horthy, who had declared that Hungary was once again a monarchy and had declared himself self-styled Regent. With Horthy's regime the pinpricks of anti-Semitism had begun to assume new proportions. One of the new government's first acts had been to pass the Numerus Clausus Law, limiting the role Jews could play in public life and restricting the entry of Jewish students into the universities.

George and Hannah, who in their early childhood felt themselves to be no different from any other Hungarian children, became gradually aware during the late 1920s of the growing tide of hostility against the nation's Jewish population. Young as they were, they felt it prudent not to overemphasize their Jewishness; some children did, and were ostracized as a result.

The growing feeling of isolation intensified after the death of Bela Senesh in May 1927. Particularly in Hannah's case, the shock of her father's death made her introverted, and she found it increasingly difficult to cement relationships with the other children round her. Nevertheless she managed to remain popular, and when she eventually entered secondary school she found herself readily accepted – a fact that was little short of astonishing, for this was a Protestant school that had taken the unprecedented and bold step of opening its doors to Catholic and Jewish children.

Although she shone in almost every academic subject she felt no sense of superiority, and took great pains to ensure that she retained good relations with both staff and pupils. Whatever frustrations she felt she poured out in the form of poetry, a love of which she had inherited from her father, and in her diary, which she began to keep at the age of thirteen.

Although by 1935 anti-Jewish demonstrations had become frequent in Hungary, so far Hannah had not experienced them personally. When it finally happened, in September 1937, it came as a bitter blow. Because of her writing prowess she was elected to the post of officer in the school literary society; soon afterwards, however, it became school policy that no Jews should hold office in any society, and she suffered the humiliation of seeing someone else elected in her place. From that moment on she became increasingly estranged from those who had once been her friends, and she began to have dark forebodings that disaster would one day overwhelm Hungary's Jews.

In 1938 the occupation by the Germans of neighbouring Austria influenced the Hungarian government, now under the leadership of Bela Imredy, to seek closer ties with the

Nazi regime. In the process Imredy, who was distinctly pro-German in outlook, agreed to the adoption of new measures to restrict the Jews still more. A Jewish bill went through parliament, prohibiting the further expansion of Jewish interests in all sectors of society, while the months that followed saw the rapid rise to power of a fascist organization known as the Arrow Cross; modelled on the lines of Hitler's SA, it shared the same doctrine as its German counterpart – a doctrine whose very foundation was anti-Semitism.

In July 1938 Hannah's brother George graduated from school and travelled to France to study textile design at the University of Lyons. It was a sad parting, for George knew that he was leaving his mother and sister to face the growing tide of persecution alone. Nevertheless there was still hope. In September 1938 the Munich Agreement was signed and the situation in Europe lost some of its tension. Although the nations of Europe still hovered on the brink of war, as long as peace reigned there was some small hope that the tide of anti-Jewish feeling might gradually recede.

As the weeks went by, however, it gradually became apparent that such hopes were barren, and at the end of October 1938 Hannah recorded in her diary that she found herself leaning more and more towards Zionism, whose most practical goal was the creation of a Jewish state in Palestine. She was doubtless influenced in her choice by her own recent experiences; her feeling now was that if the world was against the Jews, then the Jews somehow had to fight back with every means at their disposal and carve out a future for themselves in a land where they could feel secure from the terror that had been their lot for centuries.

The zeal for Zionism grew stronger, and in November Hannah told her mother that it was her dearest wish to emigrate to Palestine. Although Catherine opposed the idea at first, it soon became apparent that her daughter had become imbued with a crusading passion that nothing could stifle, and eventually she reluctantly gave in. Hannah at once applied for an immigration certificate through the Women's International Zionist Organization and wrote to the Girls' Agricultural School at Nahalal, in Palestine, seeking a position there. In May 1939 the Hungarian Government passed another Jewish bill, imposing further restrictions on the Jewish community and redistributing lands held by the Jewish middle classes. It also limited the number of Jews allowed to serve in the armed forces; those who were permitted to enter the army had to serve in front-line units, where they would be subjected to the greatest risk. While this bill was going through Parliament there was a sharp rise in anti-Jewish terrorism, culminating in the death and injury of several innocent people when a hand-grenade was thrown into a crowd emerging from a synagogue. The worst anti-Jewish atrocities during this period were committed in Carpatho-Ruthenia, which the Germans handed over to Hungary following the dismemberment of Czechoslovakia.

On 21 July 1939, four days after her eighteenth birthday, Hannah finally received her long-awaited immigration papers. There was much to be done, for she was due to be in Palestine by the end of September. Now, with the first part of her dream so close to being realized, she became tormented by fears that some last-minute snag would prevent her leaving. Black despair gripped her when, on 3 September 1939, war broke out. Although Hungary was still at peace, all routes to Palestine were abruptly closed. In desperation Hannah visited travel agents, appealed to the Jewish representative and the Office for Jewish Aid; there was nothing any of them could do. She had almost given up when she found a miraculous loophole; a group of Slovaks were given the necessary permission to travel to Palestine and she managed to attach herself to them, obtaining the necessary papers through the good offices of a

Jewish Aid representative whose father, Rabbi Miksa Weiss, had once taught Bela Senesh.

At noon the following day – 13 September 1939, just ten days after the outbreak of war – Catherine and Hannah exchanged tearful goodbyes and the girl set out for her promised land. Neither mother nor daughter had any idea what the future would hold in store for them.

Hannah arrived at Haifa on 21 September after a sea journey via Istanbul on a Rumanian steamer. The first thing that struck her was the contrast between the Palestinian Jews and those she had left behind in Hungary; there was no fear here, only a vitality, a will to progress. In this new and heady atmosphere Hannah plunged into her studies at the Nahalal Agricultural School, overlooking the valley of Jezreel. The programme was hard, the day beginning at 5.30 am and ending at 9.30 pm with only a couple of hours' free time, but she enjoyed every moment of it. Throughout her period at Nahalal Hannah continued to correspond with her mother and George, who was still in France but who was also planning to settle in Palestine. The news from Budapest was not good; crisis followed crisis as the Hungarian government became more embroiled in the affairs of Nazi Germany, and more-over – because of entry restrictions imposed by the British authorities in Palestine – it was growing harder for refugees to get out of Europe. Unrest was growing in Palestine, too; mainly as a result of the British restrictions underground movements – principally the Irgun, dedicated to the over-throw of the British in Palestine – began to flourish as never before.

In May 1940, as Hitler's victorious armies swept through France, the Hungarian government ordered general mobiliza-tion. This in itself meant further hardship for the Jews, who – although they were no longer permitted to serve in the armed forces – were formed into specially created labour units.

Several thousand strong, these labour battalions – composed of men between the ages of eighteen and forty-eight – were little more than slave gangs.

News of what was happening filtered through to Palestine, and it was now that Hannah's thoughts began to turn towards some kind of crusade. As yet it was formless; its only clear goal was to help, in some way so far undefined, the suffering people of her nation. As the weeks went by this ideal assumed an importance that transcended everything else; it was no longer enough simply to live and work in Palestine.

To the overall ideal, too, was added a sense of urgency when, in November 1940, Hungary announced her compliance with the Berlin–Rome–Tokyo Axis and stepped up her military co-operation with Germany. To Hannah, the picture was clear enough; the deeper Hungary cemented her relationship with Germany, the worse the lot of Hungarian Jewry would become.

This realization brought about a profound change in Hannah. In 1941, as the Germans swept through the Balkans and Rommel's Afrika Korps registered its first successes in the desert, the possibility of a complete Allied collapse and a sub-sequent invasion of Palestine by the Germans became a horror too great to contemplate. Oddly enough, Hannah now experi-enced a growing feeling of affection towards the British, even though she disliked their rule in Palestine. In the early part of 1941 the British stood alone against the powers of dark-ness; somehow she had to help them, and in so doing help her own people.

In June 1941 Hungary – swept by an upsurge of national-istic fervour – followed Germany's lead and declared war on the Soviet Union. Along with the fervour came still more anti-Jewish measures. In Budapest 20,000 Jews were driven from their homes and placed in detention camps on German-occupied Czech territory. In the autumn of 1941 thousands

of these unfortunates were murdered by the SS and Hungarian
police. News of the massacre was received with horror in
Palestine, and to add to Hannah's distress was the fact that
she had had no news of her mother in Budapest or George in
Lyons for some time.

By this time she was employed on a newly formed kibbutz
named Sdot Yam, situated near the old port of Caesarea some
20 miles from Haifa. In April 1942 she was recruited into the
Palmach, the offensive arm of the Haganah, the Palestinian
Jewish Self-Defence Force.

Meanwhile two things had happened that were to have
a direct influence on Hannah's activities. In the summer of
1942 a Relief and Rescue Committee was set up by the Jews
in Budapest; its main task was to smuggle Jewish refugees
from Poland, Slovakia and the Ukraine across the border into
Hungary, where they were provided with forged documents
and assimilated as Hungarian citizens. The burden was overwhelming; not only did the flood of refugees grow to massive
proportions as the summer of 1942 wore on, but the committee was desperately short of money. Nevertheless it was a step
in the right direction. Limited in scope though its activities
were, the committee was at least making an attempt to solve
some of the problems.

The second event was the rumour, soon to be tragically
substantiated, that the Germans had begun to implement
what they termed the 'final solution' with regard to the Jews:
in other words, the systematic mass-extermination of the
Jewish communities in the occupied countries. The evil ten-
tacles of the SS extermination squads were beginning to probe
into Germany's allies, too; by this time Berlin was putting
strong pressure on the Hungarian government to solve its own
'Jewish problem' by enforcing more drastic measures, and
some extremist factions in Hungary were demanding that
all Jews should be incarcerated in labour camps and ghettos.

One immediate consequence of this hardened attitude was the promulgation of an infamous order by the Hungarian Army Command; it instructed senior commanders to see that the Jewish labour battalions under their control were to be placed under conditions of extreme risk at the front. As one Hungarian commander put it: 'A good officer is one who brings back few Jews alive.'

By the Autumn of 1942 some 50,000 Jews were serving on the eastern front with the Hungarian Second Army; between 40,000 and 43,000 of them were killed when the Hungarians suffered a crushing defeat at the hands of the Red Army, many of them mown down by troops of their own side who found the Jews a convenient outlet for their frustration and despair.

At home the atrocities continued. At one *kholkhoz* 700 Jews, many of them suffering from typhoid, were forced on to the roof of a large stable by Hungarian police. During the night fire broke out in the stable; many Jews tried to save themselves by jumping into the courtyard, only to be shot by Hungarian soldiers. Terrified, the remaining Jews huddled together on the roof of the stable until it finally collapsed into the flames below.

The problem of doing something to help Hungary's Jews was fast becoming a race against time; for Hannah, it was now a question of translating her ideals into firm action. Her chance came in February 1943, when a young man named Yonah Rosen visited Sdot Yam. Rosen, who was also a Palmach member, told Hannah that the Haganah was forming a parachute mission composed of Palestinian Jews. Training, equipment and aircraft would be provided by the British, and in exchange for this the first task of the mission's members, when they were eventually parachuted into enemy territory, would be to set up escape routes for shot-down Allied airmen or escaping prisoners-of-war. Once this had been accomplished they would be free to do what they could to help Jewish refugees to get away from the Nazis.

Hannah gave no thought to the fact that the parachutists would be embarking on what amounted to a suicide mission; this was what she had been waiting for. She volunteered immediately, and in May 1943 she was called for an interview before a joint panel of British officers and Haganah members – a strange combination, since the Haganah was an illegal organization.

The interview was followed by long months of waiting. It was not until December 1943 that she learned that she had been accepted and was ordered to report to Tel Aviv to begin her training. The headquarters of the training school were situated on a kibbutz named Ramat Hakovesh; although under British command, most of the instructors were Palmach officers. Everything was carried out under conditions of strict secrecy; such secrecy, in fact, that a British military police patrol, unaware of the true nature of Ramat Hakovesh, once raided the kibbutz and carried out a search for illegal arms!

There were thirty-two volunteers in all – twenty drawn from the various kibbutzim and twelve from Jews serving in the British forces. Besides Hannah there were two other girls; one failed to complete the tough course and the other, Chaviva Reik, was eventually parachuted into Czechoslovakia, where she was captured and executed.

At Ramat Hakovesh Hannah learned a new trade – the trade of killing. She learned how to end a man's life silently, with a knife, or noisily with a Sten gun, a Tommy gun, a German Schmeisser and a Colt .45. She learned how to kill with her bare hands – a possibility that revolted her – and to crush someone's skull with a small and deadly club used by Israeli shepherds since biblical times. Then, in January 1944, the course moved to a British Army establishment at Ramat David to begin parachute training, carrying out a series of five 'live' jumps – one at night – in the space of a week. While at Ramat David the mission was officially incorporated into the Royal Air Force, its members being made NCOs and later commissioned.

Halfway through her course Hannah experienced a fresh upheaval in her life; her brother George arrived at Haifa, having made his way to Palestine via Spain. The meeting between brother and sister was both joyous and painful; Hannah was bursting to tell George of her mission, but she was sworn to absolute secrecy. Instead she told him that she had joined the RAF as a radio operator. After they parted, she wept for hours. She knew that she might never see him again.

The mission was now split up into several groups, who were assigned various objectives in occupied Europe according to their nationalities. The Hungarian group, comprising Hannah, Dafne, Berdichev and Rosen, were sent to Egypt to carry out intelligence training. In February, while they were in Cairo, they learned of a German plan to carry out a full-scale occupation of Hungary. For the nation's million Jews the race against time was becoming desperate. It was with a sense of relief that, early in March, Hannah and her colleagues were flown to Brindisi; the mission – the crusade – was getting under way at last.

They parachuted into the night sky over Yugoslavia, where they were to link up with a partisan group before crossing the Hungarian border. The drop and the landing were faultless. It was in the early hours of 15 March 1944.

That same day German troops marched into Budapest. The column of troops and armour stretched for over a mile. Among it was an SS unit; its designation was *Sondereinsatzkommando*, or Special Operations Group. It was commanded by a fair-haired, cold-eyed *Obersturmbannführer* named Adolf Eichmann, and its task was murder.

For three months Hannah and her comrades, bitterly frus-

trated at the delay, roved the forests and mountains of Yugoslavia with the partisans. On one occasion, in a border village,
they came close to death when the partisan unit was ambushed by a German patrol. They escaped by dashing down
a slope, with partisans and villagers being cut down on all
sides, and hid in some bushes until the danger was over.

Early in June, with visions of wandering aimlessly across
Yugoslavia for the rest of the war, Hannah persuaded the
others that they ought to leave the partisans and head for the
border. On 9 June, as they approached the frontier under
cover of some woods, they met a group of Hungarian Jews
heading in the opposite direction. The men were terrified,
and from them Hannah learned of the horror that was engulf-
ing her country. Eichmann's *Sondereinsatzkommando* was
doing its terrible work with cold-blooded efficiency; every
day thousands of Jews were leaving Budapest in railway cattle
trucks, their destination the infamous death camp at Auschwitz. By the end of May the daily total had risen to 12,000,
and it was planned to deport over 100,000 people by the end
of July.

Still sick with horror, Hannah and the others slipped across
the border, striking out across country towards Budapest.
They were accompanied by two members of the group they
had encountered, an underground worker named Kallos and
a French non-Jew, an escaped prisoner-of-war named Jacques
Tissandier. The mission now split up, heading for the capital
by different routes. It was hard going; Hannah, with Kallos
and Tissandier, had to swim the River Drava, swollen by the
spring torrents that flowed from the mountains. They made
the crossing several times, battling against the current, to ferry
across Hannah's bulky radio transmitter piece by piece.

At dawn, shivering with cold after crossing three more
rivers, they sighted a village. While Tissandier and Hannah
hid in some reeds, Kallos went on ahead to investigate. On the

way back he was stopped by a Hungarian police patrol. Trembling with fear, he reached into his pocket as though to produce his identity paper. Instead he dragged out a pistol and shot himself through the head.

Hannah and Tissandier saw the whole tragedy from their vantage-point in the reeds. They saw, too, the policemen search Kallos's pockets and produce a set of earphones – part of Hannah's radio transmitter.

They hid in the reeds for three hours, not daring to move, until they saw a German patrol marching down the road towards them. Slowly, they inched their way through the reeds until they reached the shelter of a nearby wood, where they buried their guns and radio equipment. As they worked they could hear shouted orders in German, and realized that the wood was being surrounded.

The frightened couple crouched in the undergrowth, listening to the sounds of the search coming steadily closer. At the last moment they embraced one another, hoping that the Germans would take them for lovers and ignore them. Endless minutes ticked by; there was the noise of boots, crackling through the twigs and leaves. The sound stopped abruptly and they looked up into the black muzzle of a Schmeisser.

They were handcuffed and taken to the police headquarters in Szombathely, where they were confronted with the bloodstained corpse of Kallos. An hour later, a German NCO came in, triumphantly bearing Hannah's radio transmitter and weapons. The enemy had been thorough.

During the next two days Hannah was interrogated ceaselessly and whipped on the soles of her feet and palms of her hands until she lost consciousness. Finally, hardly able to walk, she was placed under heavy guard and put on a train for Budapest. On the way she tried to throw herself from the compartment, but the guards were quicker and she was seized just in time.

As the train drew into Budapest she closed the little book of French poetry that her captors had allowed her to bring with her and laid it aside on the seat. No one took any notice, not even when she left it behind as they disembarked. The Germans had no way of knowing that the book contained the key to the radio code that was to have been used by the Hungarian mission. Hannah had not committed any of it to memory; now she could not reveal it, even under the most terrible torture.

In Budapest she was taken to the Horthy Miklos Street Military Prison. There, for weeks on end, she was subjected to one beating after another. Her feet and hands became unusable lumps of raw meat; she was stripped naked and flogged until her body was criss-crossed with vicious cuts; her hair was pulled out in fistfuls and her teeth shattered into bloody splinters. And still she refused to talk.

Outside her grim prison walls, across the breadth of Hungary, the atrocities continued as Eichmann's murderers deported the Jews in their thousands. At one town nearly a hundred courageous people lay on the railway line in an attempt to stop a deportee train from leaving. The SS raked them with machine-guns and the train moved forward over the bodies. On average four trains a day left Hungary for the death camps; each train carried 3,000 souls. By the end of June 1944 382,000 Jews had made the one-way trip to oblivion, while the deportation of 200,000 more was planned for July.

At the end of June Hannah was visited in prison by her mother, Catherine. It was a terrible meeting. Until the military authorities informed her that her daughter was being held, Catherine had believed her to be safe in Palestine. At first Catherine hardly recognized the girl; Hannah's face was bruised and swollen, her once-smooth skin blotched and coarse, her hands broken and claw-like. The two women broke down completely. Later Hannah realized that her mother's presence had been a clumsy attempt by the police to break what was left of her resistance. It failed.

Later that day Catherine was also arrested by the SS and placed in the same prison as Hannah. In a strange way it brought her reassurance; although she was not allowed to meet Hannah, she managed to catch occasional glimpses of the girl as she walked round the prison yard during her daily exercise period.

Hannah's daily interrogations continued. The beatings had all but stopped now, but the constant mental strain was taking its toll. When she returned to her cell Hannah managed to find solace in making rag dolls for the many children who hung round the prison : sons and daughters of inmates who, without a home, had been shuttled from camp to camp and prison to prison. Also, every evening, in defiance of prison regulations, she stood at her cell window and called out snippets of news she had picked up during the day. It brought solace to the other prisoners, and although she was frequently beaten for it, Hannah refused to stop.

In July she passed on one piece of information that set the walls ringing with the prisoners' cheers. It had been kept a closely guarded secret for several weeks, but she had heard it in the form of a chance remark from a German soldier. The Allies had landed in France; the Germans were on the retreat in both east and west.

The weeks wore on, and with them came a relaxation in the harsh treatment meted out to Hannah. She even began to hope that she might be transferred to Kistarcsa, an internment camp where conditions were less strict. Even the interrogations ceased in August. There were disturbing rumours that all Hungarian prisoners under German jurisdiction – which included Hannah – were to be deported, but she pushed them to the back of her mind and tried to forget them. Soon afterwards she was placed in a cell next to her mother, and the two women were able to talk in whispers. Then, on the night of 10 September, the hopes that Hannah and Catherine had cherished for so many weeks were brutally shattered. Catherine awoke in the night to the sounds of a commotion in the corridors, with the clatter of boots and people sobbing. Eichmann's familiars were once more at work, dragging people at random from the cells and out into the darkness.

When morning came Hannah too was gone: no one would say where. In fact she had been taken to Budapest's Conti Street Prison, where she was to be detained pending her trial for treason. It was held on 28 October 1944, and was a complete travesty. Although it was in the hands of a Hungarian judge and jury, Hannah had no doubt what the outcome would be. The sinister shadow of Eichmann loomed too large over the Hungarian authorities for them to dare to pass anything other than the death sentence.

On the morning of 7 November 1944 Hannah Senesh was taken from her cell and bound to a wooden stake in the prison yard. She refused the blindfold they offered her. A minute later the grey walls echoed to a crash of rifle fire.

In the cells the other prisoners stood silently to attention, the tears streaming down their faces. It was their only way of paying tribute to a heroine.

The following day, the Red Army battered its way into southern Hungary and the race for Budapest began. Ahead of the advancing Russians, Eichmann's execution squads rounded up all the Jews they could find and herded them on a terrible forced march into Austria. Catherine Senesh was among them, but she was one of the lucky ones. She managed to escape and return to Budapest, hiding in a convent until the Russians occupied the city.

Adolf Eichmann escaped the clutches of the Allies in the whirlpool of confusion that reigned at the end of the war.

Fifteen years later, masquerading under the name of Ricardo Clemens, he was captured in Rio de Janeiro by a group of dedicated Israeli Nazi-hunters. He was smuggled into Israel, tried and executed.

One life for the lives of half a million Hungarian Jews; it was a hollow triumph.

4 Last Flight from Berlin

IT IS A FACT that courage knows no national frontiers. It is also a fact that, at the end of a war, the valorous deeds of the victor are extolled time and again, while those of the vanquished are swallowed up in the chaos of defeat. Yet in the story of the German armed forces between 1939 and 1945 there were many instances of great individual bravery that have gone unrecorded. It is for this reason that I have chosen, to symbolize these forgotten enemy heroes, to tell the story of the famous woman pilot Hanna Reitsch, whose courage and dedication during five long years of war would have been legendary in any language.

It was 26 April 1945.

After five bitter years of war Hitler's 'Thousand-Year Reich' was crumbling into blazing ruin. In the *Führerbunker* under the Reichs-Chancellery the madman who had plunged the world into chaos and ended the lives of millions of people pushed little coloured counters round a huge chart-board, deploying non-existent divisions to break the Russian ring of steel that surrounded Berlin. The end of his own life was days away and he was already a phantom, his face pale and haggard, his hands trembling uncontrollably.

Over the suburbs of the hell that was Berlin a light aircraft flew : a slow, insect-like Fieseler Storch observation plane. It cruised low over the burning rubble, over the endless columns of drab vehicles with their red stars, over the T-34 tanks crunching their way over the fallen masonry towards the heart of the city. It passed over the Grünewald, its wheels brushing the treetops to avoid detection by the swarms of Russian fighters that ruled the sky over the capital. From all sides lances of fire rose up to meet the little aircraft, coning it in a deadly spider's web of tracer, cannon shells, small-arms fire and flak bursts. Jagged chunks of white-hot metal ripped through the fabric of its wings and fuselage, and the plane's occupants measured their life expectancy in seconds.

There were two of them, their faces masks of horror as they saw the destruction of Berlin unfolding below them. One was Colonel-General Ritter von Greim, of the Luftwaffe High Command; the other was a slight, fair-haired woman, Fraülein Hanna Reitsch.

For Hanna, the road to that murderous cauldron of Berlin in the spring of 1945 had been adventurous and full of danger. It began when, as a child, she cycled to the airfield at Grunau near her home in Silesia to watch gliders wheeling among the clouds; later, on leaving school, she too experienced the joy of silent flight at that same training-field. She worked hard to perfect her natural flying ability, and in due course became a gliding instructor. Later while completing her studies at medical college, she also learned to fly powered aircraft.

Hanna's father was a doctor and his dearest wish was that his daughter should follow in his footsteps, but it was soon apparent that her heart lay elsewhere. Flying – and particularly gliding – was her whole life. She took part in international soaring contests all over the world, trained glider pilots in Finland and, after a course at the Civil Airways Training School in Stettin, joined the staff of the German Institute for Glider Research in 1935.

From now on her rise to fame was rapid. She tested gliders, flew the fighters and bombers that were finding their way to the embryo squadrons of the new Luftwaffe, and set up a record by making the first ever indoor flight in a helicopter, at the Deutschlandhalle in Berlin during the International Motor Show of 1937.

The outbreak of war in 1939 found her involved in the testing of troop-carrying gliders, work that culminated, in May 1940, in an assault by German glider-borne troops on the Belgian defences on the western front. Later, during the period of the Battle of Britain, she flew a variety of aircraft fitted with experimental equipment designed to cut the cables of barrage balloons. This involved flying deliberately into balloon cables, and on one occasion a cable through which her aircraft's wing had just sliced flicked back like a whiplash and shattered her propeller, almost tearing the engine from its mountings. With her machine riddled by metal fragments,

Hanna managed to make a forced landing in a field. For her cable-cutting exploits she was awarded the Iron Cross, Second Class.

Shortly afterwards, because of her extensive gliding experience, she was selected to test-fly the unpowered version of the Messerschmitt Me-163 rocket fighter. She made four successful flights; then, on the fifth, she ran into trouble.

As usual, she was towed to altitude behind a twin-engined Me-110 over the airfield near Regensburg. Everything went well until she pulled the handle that was supposed to release the Me-163's undercarriage – a two-wheel trolley that was used only on take-off, the aircraft landing on its own built-in skid. Suddenly the 163 started to shudder violently; the undercarriage had stuck. There was nothing for it but to gain as much height as possible, then try out the aircraft's controls to see if they still worked properly and glide down for an emergency landing.

The Me-110 towed her up to 10,000 feet and she cast off, gliding down in wide circles until she was in a position to begin her final approach to the field. As she crossed the boundary she side-slipped to lose some surplus height – and the machine stalled, plummeting earthwards like a stone. There was no time even to think. Instinctively, she curled herself up into a ball as the earth reared up in front of her. Then came a fearful jolt, a rending crash – and silence.

The aircraft had turned a complete somersault and come to rest the right way up. At first Hanna thought she had escaped uninjured, but then she felt blood streaming down her face. Even now her pilot's training took charge; pulling a notepad and pencil from her pocket, she made a sketch and notes of the events leading up to the crash. Only then did she lose consciousness.

She had sustained four skull fractures, involving compression of the brain, displacement of the upper jawbone and separation of the bones of the nose. She was, in fact, extremely lucky to be alive. She remained in hospital in Regensburg for over five months before the doctors finally saw fit to discharge her in March 1943.

Typically, she refused to enter a long convalescence, returning at once to the Me-163 test programme. During this period she also spent three weeks on the Russian front as the guest of Colonel-General von Greim, visiting Luftwaffe units and several times coming under heavy Russian fire as she toured the German forward anti-aircraft positions. The horrors of the eastern front made a deep impression on her, and it was with considerable relief that she returned to Germany in December 1943.

It was not long before she became involved in the most dangerous project of her entire flying career. Towards the end of the year she was one of a group of people – including Luftwaffe officers, test pilots and civilian officials – that met under conditions of strict secrecy at the Institute of Aviation Medicine in Rechlin. Every member of the group had two things in common : each was dedicated to Germany; and each knew that – slowly but surely – Germany was losing the war. The Allies had already invaded Sicily and Italy, and it could only be a question of time before they attempted an invasion of Western Europe.

The only hope of disrupting such an invasion would be by means of massive air attacks on the Allied convoys as they approached the beaches. It was clear, however, that the Luftwaffe's dwindling resources would not be equal to the task – unless new and revolutionary tactics were used. Such tactics were being proposed by the Rechlin group, every member of which was prepared to sacrifice his own life deliberately to achieve victory. The group was proposing, in fact, to form a Luftwaffe suicide squadron. The idea was to use a piloted version of the famous V-1 flying bomb. This would be carried aloft under the wing of a bomber, then released and steered to its target by the suicide pilot. It would be a very simple affair, with no undercarriage and only the most rudimentary of cockpits. After all, its designers pointed out, it would be used only for one trip.

Nevertheless the piloted V-1 – known as the Reichenberg – had to be test-flown, and Hanna Reitsch was one of the pilots who volunteered to carry out this highly dangerous task. The first test flight was hardly calculated to inspire confidence. Flown by a Luftwaffe officer, the Reichenberg was released from its Heinkel ' mother plane ' without difficulty and entered a series of gentle turns, but then – just as it seemed everything was going well – the aircraft went into a steep dive, hit the ground and blew up. The following day a second Reichenberg also crashed, but the pilot miraculously escaped with his life.

Then it was Hanna's turn – and to everyone's astonishment and relief her first flight in the piloted V-1 passed without incident. The V-1 handled better than she had expected and she made a perfect touch-down on the machine's landing skid. The next flight, however, was not so trouble free. At the moment of release from under the bomber's wing the two aircraft collided, crumpling the V-1's tail and almost tearing it off. By some miracle the controls still worked, and Hanna was able to make an emergency landing with nothing worse than a severe shaking.

On another occasion she was testing a V-1 with a water-tank built into its fuselage to simulate the explosive charge the weapon would eventually carry. This water had to be released through a special vent before landing, otherwise the extra weight would cause the aircraft to break up. During the test flight Hanna pulled the lever that operated the vent – and found to her horror that it was frozen solid. The heavily laden V-1 dropped like a stone, and in desperation she tore at the lever until her hands were bloody as the earth sped towards her. At last, with only a couple of hundred feet to go, the lever jerked free; the water poured from the tank and she was able to make a normal landing. Once again, luck had been on her side.

For Germany, however, the sands were fast running out. In June 1944, while testing of the piloted V-1 continued, the Allies went ashore in Normandy. Not long afterwards, the suicide group was disbanded.

In April 1945, after a spell in hospital recovering from injuries sustained during an American air-raid on Berlin, Hanna received a message from Colonel-General von Greim, ordering her to report to his headquarters in Munich to undertake a special mission. It involved flying into the heart of Berlin – which by this time was completely encircled by Russian forces – to receive orders from Adolf Hitler in the Chancellery.

In the early hours of 26 April Hanna and von Greim flew to Rechlin, where they learned that no German aircraft had succeeded in penetrating the Russian defences and flying into Berlin for over two days. One of the city's airfields, Gatow, was still in German hands, but it was surrounded by the Russians and under continual shellfire. No one knew whether enough of its runways remained to allow an aircraft to land.

The plan was to fly into Gatow, and from there make the final 'hop' to the Chancellery in the city centre. If they were to break through the ring of Russian anti-aircraft guns and fighters speed was essential, so for the flight into Gatow it was decided to use the fastest aircraft available – a Focke-Wulf 190 fighter, specially modified to carry a passenger. The aircraft was to be flown by a Luftwaffe sergeant, with von Greim occupying the second seat. Hanna presented something of a problem, since there was no room for three people in the narrow cockpit. In the end she wormed her way feet first into a tiny, tunnel-like space in the rear of the fuselage, where she lay in complete darkness surrounded by oxygen cylinders and other odds and ends.

It was the most terrifying flight of her life. The noise was terrific; she was totally unable to move and the metal objects that surrounded her pressed painfully into her body. The flight to Gatow lasted thirty minutes, and seemed like an eternity. Once Hanna thought her last moment had come when the aircraft went into a screaming power-dive; later she learned that the pilot had been avoiding Russian fighters.

They landed at Gatow amid a storm of Russian gunfire. Every aircraft on the field had been knocked out except one, a Fieseler Storch observation machine. Hanna and von Greim took off in it at 6 pm, heading for the Brandenburg Gate, where they hoped to find a space big enough to land in. Since Hanna had no experience of flying under fire, von Greim insisted on piloting the little aircraft – but Hanna made sure that she could reach the controls over his shoulder.

It was just as well that she did so. As the little machine skimmed through the murderous fire over the Grünewald, there was a sudden deafening bang and a yellow flame streaked back from the engine. At the same instant von Greim shouted that he had been hit; an armour-piercing bullet had smashed through his right foot. A moment later he slumped to one side, unconscious.

Hanna at once reached across his inert body, grabbing the controls and fighting to keep the aircraft twisting and turning to avoid the worst of the Russian fire. Outside the cockpit the whole sky seemed to be in flames as shell after shell exploded, sending wicked splinters slicing through wings and fuselage. White-hot bullets shattered the perspex of the cockpit, but by a miracle none of them struck Hanna. With sick fear, she noticed rivers of fuel pouring from bullet-torn wing tanks; all it needed was a single incendiary bullet and the aircraft would disintegrate in a ball of flame. But the sturdy little machine flew on, still answering the controls, over the shattered suburbs of Berlin.

Gradually, as she neared the city centre, the Russian fire died away. Now, however, the smoke from burning buildings mushroomed up in sulphurous yellow clouds, making it impossible to see ahead. The ruins flashed past, dangerously close, as she followed her compass blindly, heading for a landmark she knew well : a tall anti-aircraft tower that stood next to the broad highway running east–west through Berlin. The aircraft lurched and jolted in the turbulence that rose from the fires below, and her task of controlling it was made more difficult by von Greim, who kept regaining consciousness for a few seconds at a time and convulsively seizing the stick. Each time Hanna had to fight him off, and they came perilously close to diving into the sea of rubble and fire.

At last, almost exhausted, she saw the flak tower looming up through the smoke, with the road beyond it. She turned east, following the bomb-cratered ribbon of concrete until she sighted the Brandenburg Gate. She touched down close by the famous landmark and helped von Greim – who by this time had regained his senses – out of the aircraft. She bound his shattered foot as best she could and they sat there among the piles of fallen masonry for a long time, choking in the swirling smoke, before a German Army lorry appeared, threading its way through the debris.

They were driven to Hitler's bunker at the Chancellery, where von Greim's foot was operated on immediately. Afterwards, with the general still on a stretcher, they were taken for an audience with Hitler. It was only now that they learned the reason behind their summons to Berlin : Hitler believed that Hermann Goering, the commander-in-chief of the Luftwaffe, had betrayed him – and von Greim was to be appointed his successor, with immediate promotion to the rank of field-marshal.

The irony of the situation did not escape Hanna. Von Greim was now commander of an air force that no longer existed – and the divisions that Hitler still expected to come to the rescue of Berlin no longer existed either. With the thunder of Russian artillery all round him, he was living in a world of fantasy that no amount of reasoning could destroy.

Then came the final irony. After two days in the nightmare unreality of the bunker, von Greim and Hanna were once again ordered to report to Hitler, who told them that he had received news of an impending Russian attack on the bunker. Hanna and the general were to leave at once, von Greim with orders to organize an all-out attack on the Russian forces that threatened the Chancellery. Another light aircraft, an Arado, had managed to land on the east–west highway and was waiting for them.

They stepped out of the bunker into an inferno of flame and smoke, made more nightmarish by the banshee wail of shells that were erupting all round. An armoured car was waiting for them, and they set off on their eerie journey through the lurid darkness. The shattered streets seemed deserted, and apart from the flickering fires the only movement came from the ghostly beams of Russian searchlights positioned at the eastern end of the central highway.

They found the aircraft parked behind a blast-proof wall next to a 400-yard stretch of road that was so far clear of shell craters. Its pilot – the same man who had flown them into Gatow three days earlier – had brought the machine down unharmed, even though the road had been raked by Russian gunfire. Now, with Hanna and von Greim on board, he taxied cautiously out and pointed the Arado's nose towards the smoke that swirled over the highway.

The aircraft took off and headed towards the Brandenburg Gate, flying between the ruined buildings to avoid the Russian searchlights. Tracer bullets flickered past, but they were wide of the mark. After a mile, the pilot climbed steeply and entered a bank of cloud, which sheltered them until they were clear of the dying city. They landed at Rechlin at 3 o'clock in the morning, their nostrils still clogged with the stench of smoke and death.

The last day of April found them at Lübeck, where von Greim conferred with other senior officers. That same evening, they learned that Adolf Hitler was dead.

Nevertheless von Greim was still determined to carry out his last order, and a day later he and Hanna flew to Zell-am-See in Austria, where the general hoped to assemble what was left of the Luftwaffe. They were still there when, on 9 May, Germany signed an unconditional surrender. Soon afterwards, both were captured by the Americans.

For Hanna it was the start of a confinement that was to last for fifteen months, before she was eventually released in August 1946. The Americans treated her with considerable suspicion – an understandable reaction, for she was a leading member of the Nazi Party and had enjoyed the confidence of Hitler and his closest advisers.

It soon became apparent to her captors, however, that her first and only love was flying; and in the narrow confines of her cell she lived only for the day when she could once again take to the air – a dream she ultimately realized.

She is still flying today – a living symbol of courage that continues to inspire aviators not only in her homeland but throughout the world.

5 The Auschwitz Heroines

AMONG ALL THE HORROR that arose from the grim years of World War Two, one name more than any other is calculated to arouse the deepest feelings of revulsion and loathing against the Nazi creed: Auschwitz.

To some extent, every woman who suffered in Auschwitz or one of the other death camps was a heroine; yet two names stand out as a symbol of courage, fortitude and resistance under the most evil and horrifying circumstances ever devised by men.

This is the story of Mala Zimetbaum and Rosa Robota, whose bravery and devotion were a source of inspiration to thousands of tragic, doomed people who were the victims of Hitler's 'final solution'.

Mala Zimetbaum was born in Brzesko, Poland, in 1920. When she was eight years old her family, terrified by the growing wave of anti-Jewish feeling, emigrated to Belgium and settled in Antwerp. They were still there when, in May 1940, the terror reached out to engulf them with the German occupation of France and the Low Countries.

Soon after they had completed their occupation of Belgium the Germans began, with fearful speed and efficiency, to deport train-loads of Jews from the country's major towns and cities. Many of the victims still managed to joke and smile despite their fear as they were herded on to the cattle trucks, believing that their lot would be forced labour at the worst; at this stage in the war, the full horror of Hitler's extermination camps had yet to be revealed.

Mala was more fortunate than many of her friends in that she managed to evade the German 'special squads' for two years. However she was finally rounded up with two thousand others in 1942 and taken to a collecting centre at Malines, where she was pushed on to an airless, overcrowded train to the accompaniment of curses and blows from rifle butts. The train was bound for a place whose name had already spread like a ripple of horror through Europe's Jewish population: Auschwitz.

For nearly a year Mala clung doggedly to life in the death camp while starvation and brutality took their toll of those with whom she had left Belgium. Once again luck seemed to favour her; because of her ability to speak several languages the Germans selected her to be an interpreter and runner, which meant that she was able to obtain extra rations. Just as important, she could move freely from one part of the camp to another, a privilege that was denied to the other prisoners. Despite the appalling risk of death if she were caught, she used her position to smuggle messages and small packets of food or medicine into the various compounds, and in 1943 she became involved in an embryo underground movement that some of the prisoners were beginning to organize.

One of the tasks allocated to Mala was to visit the camp hospital daily and work out a duty roster for those pronounced fit enough to work. Many were so weak that they could hardly stand, and these Mala assigned to the lightest possible duties. The German guards also visited the hospital each day to make what was known as the ' selection '. Anyone unlucky enough to be on their list went to the gas chamber. Mala usually knew when these visits were due to take place, and she made a point of going to the hospital beforehand to warn others, helping all but the most hopeless cases to get out of the building and lose themselves in the anonymity of the camp. No one will ever know how many lives she saved in this way.

She herself grew steadily weaker as the months went by, and in 1944 she came close to total collapse. It happened in May, when up to 12,000 Jews from Hungary began to arrive at Auschwitz every day – and all but a handful were sent straight to the gas chambers. Although the whole camp was enveloped in a pall of greasy smoke from the overworked crematoria and the continual stench of burning bodies, most of the new arrivals seemed unable to comprehend what was happening to them. After being segregated from the men the women and children stood there naked, in bewildered groups, patiently waiting their turn for what they had been told was to be a communal bath. The cries of the children were hideous, mingling with the screamed orders of the SS guards and frequent shots as someone stepped out of line and was gunned down.

It went on day after day, week after week, until finally Mala could stand it no longer. She knew that she had to get out of Auschwitz, or lose her sanity and the will to live. But escape from the hell camp was virtually impossible; she knew of several people who had tried it, but all had been captured and shot out of hand by the SS guards or torn to pieces by the vicious guard dogs.

Nevertheless she was determined to make the attempt – but she knew that she could never do it alone. Then, soon after the plan had begun to form in her mind, she came into contact with a Pole from the men's camp named Edek Galinski. Like her, he was bent on escape, but – more to the point – he had been in the camp since 1940 and had actually helped to build it, which meant that he knew every inch of its layout, including the guarded perimeter. Moreover in his work as a mechanic he was often in touch with civilian workmen from outside, who were brought specially into the camp to carry out tasks that the Germans considered too important to be undertaken by prisoners. Through these workmen he had succeeded in establishing a number of contacts beyond the barbed wire.

Galinski's plan envisaged dressing up as an SS guard and boldly walking out of the main gate, accompanied by a prisoner – a combination that, he hoped, would give the impression that he was escorting one of the inmates to a work detail outside the camp. In return for a promise that she would play the part of the prisoner, Mala agreed to steal a special permit – required by anyone leaving Auschwitz – during one of her routine visits to the guardroom.

The date they fixed for the hazardous attempt was 24 June 1944. It was a Saturday, a day that was usually quieter than normal since many of the guards went off duty at noon and the guardroom was consequently undermanned. Since she was

well known round the camp, Mala decided to make her bid
for freedom dressed as a man and to carry something – bucket
or washing bowl – on her head to hide her face.

Shortly before noon on the appointed day Mala and
Galinski made a secret rendezvous and made their way inde-
pendently towards the guardroom, with Mala leading. Beneath
her striped prison garments, fastened round her waist, she
carried a dress that she had fashioned laboriously from scraps
of material during the past weeks. It was shabby, patchy
and it made her look like a tramp, but it would pass any but
the closest inspection and was far less conspicuous than her
prison clothing. Galinski's home-made SS uniform had
already been hidden by the girl in a nearby washroom.

Slowly Mala walked across the compound towards the
guardroom. At exactly 12 o'clock the German duty officer
emerged and roared off through the gates on his motorcycle,
no doubt eagerly looking forward to his afternoon off. Near
the steps of the guardroom stood three girls, runners like
Mala, and friends who had been let in on her secret. One of
them now gave a nod, indicating that the coast was clear.
They stayed where they were, ostensibly ready to run messages
for the Germans but prepared to give timely warning to Mala
at the first sign of danger.

Mala entered the guardroom. There was only one occupant,
a female SS overseer. Mala knew her well, right down to the
fact that the woman was an alcoholic, and had come prepared
with a bottle of vodka. Surprised, the overseer thanked the
Jewish girl and at once proceeded to empty the contents of
the bottle down her throat.

Mala made herself as inconspicuous as possible and waited
until the German woman collapsed face down on the table
in a drunken stupor. Then she went to the washroom and
changed into her man's clothing. A minute later Galinski also
arrived and put on the SS uniform. Then the two left the

building and made their way towards the perimeter, Mala, with the washing bowl on her head, keeping a few paces behind Galinski as was usual when a prisoner accompanied a guard.

Mala's heart pounded in fear as they approached the gate, which was set in an electrified wire fence with watch-towers, armed with machine-guns and manned by SS guards, at 50-yard intervals. Fortunately the gate was open and the bored-looking sentry – one of a contingent recently posted to the camp, who had not yet had time to familiarize himself with the officers – spared them hardly a glance as they went through.

With this obstacle behind them they now found themselves in the outer perimeter – a strip of barren earth that surrounded the entire camp complex and was patrolled constantly by guards and dogs. Once again luck was with them; there were plenty of working parties moving round the perimeter and no one took any notice as they walked on.

Restraining the impulse to run, expecting at any moment to hear a shout and the crackle of gunfire, they passed one of Auschwitz's many prison compounds. Beyond it lay a corn-field. At its edge they paused, snatched a hasty glance backwards, then dived for shelter among the stalks.

Back in the camp, it was several hours before their escape was discovered – when an irate officer called in at the guard-room on his return to duty and kicked the chair from under the drunken overseer. The whole camp was in an uproar. Sirens wailed, squads of prisoners were counted and recounted, every possible hiding-place was searched. The whole country-side was alerted and patrols with tracker dogs scoured the area.

They found nothing, and as the days went by Mala's friends found growing hope that she and Galinski had got away. Her three fellow-runners were arrested and accused of helping her to escape, but they protested their innocence and escaped the death sentence; instead they were stripped of their privileges and sent to work in a labour gang.

A week passed; ten days. Then the blow fell. Word reached the prisoners that Mala and Galinski had been recaptured close to the Czech border and were now back at Auschwitz under interrogation. At first they refused to believe it; then Mala herself smuggled a message to them from her cell, and there was no longer any doubt.

Mala and Galinski were interrogated by an SS thug named Wilhelm Boger, who was later to be sentenced to life imprisonment by the Allies. Known as the 'devil of Auschwitz', he was a specialist in the most refined tortures, and used them all in an attempt to make Mala and her colleague reveal who had helped them to escape. Throughout their ordeal, they remained silent.

On the evening of 22 August 1944 the Jewish prisoners were ordered to assemble in the compound of Camp B at Auschwitz-Birkenau. A few minutes later Mala appeared, together with the head of work details, a man named Riters, and the commander of the women's camp, Frau Mandel. The latter stepped forward and began to read something from a paper; it was Mala's death sentence.

Suddenly the Jewish girl produced something from the folds of her prison uniform: a razor. In horrified silence the others watched as she began to slash at her wrists, determined to cheat the Germans of their vengeance. Then Riters noticed the expressions on the prisoners' faces, swung round and seized Mala's arm. She struck out at him with all her strength, spraying blood over his face and uniform, before she was overpowered. Then they dragged her away, shouting words of encouragement to the others.

They took her to the camp hospital and bandaged her wounds. Then they beat her. Still she screamed at them, hurling abuse and promising them that their turn would soon come. Finally they taped her mouth with adhesive to stifle her cries and threw her, still living, on to a wooden cart. A few minutes later they hurled her into the furnace of the crematorium.

Today there is a plaque on the house in Antwerp where Mala lived. It reads: 'To Mala Zimetbaum, Symbol of Solidarity, Murdered by the Nazis in Auschwitz, 22 August 1944'. A brief epitaph for a valiant girl.

On 7 October 1944, six weeks after Mala's death, a tremendous explosion rocked the women's Camp B at Auschwitz-Birkenau. It was 3 o'clock in the afternoon and the inmates looked at one another in disbelief. A huge column of smoke and flame was rising from one of the crematoria.

All hell was let loose as the guards charged about in complete confusion, shouting orders and curses and lashing out at the prisoners, forcing them into their barrack blocks under the menace of their sub-machine-guns and quite obviously terrified that a full-scale revolt was under way. Within minutes fresh detachments of soldiers were on their way to the camp; these were seasoned regular troops of the Wehrmacht, fresh from duty on the Russian front, and now they surrounded the crematorium and opened fire with heavy machine-guns. A few scattered revolver shots replied, then the Wehrmacht troops and SS charged the building. The other inmates cowered in terror in their huts, and wondered what was happening.

One person knew: a twenty-year-old Polish girl named Rosa Robota. She was eighteen years old when, in September 1939, the Germans occupied her home town of Ciechanow, and within days she became involved in an active underground movement centred on the Jewish ghetto. Then, in November 1942, the Germans razed the ghetto to the ground and shipped its inhabitants to the Auschwitz and Treblinka death camps.

At Auschwitz Rosa was employed in the clothing store. She had a bitter hatred of the Germans and a deep thirst for revenge, for the rest of her family had been sent to the gas chambers, and she was enthusiastic when the Jewish underground movement in Auschwitz asked her if she would help them. The resistance workers were planning a general uprising in the camp, which was to be signalled by the destruction of the crematoria and gas chambers, and for this they needed explosives and detonators. The problem was that the resistance leaders had so far found it impossible to make contact with the group of Jewish girls who worked in the gunpowder section of a nearby factory, for they worked under strict surveillance and any contact with them was punishable by death. Since several of the girls came from Rosa's home town and she encountered them occasionally in the clothing store, she was thought to be the ideal person to make the initial approach.

Rosa readily agreed. Here at last was the chance to translate some of her pent-up anger and frustration into firm action. Before long she had assembled a team of a dozen girls, all of whom worked in the munitions factory; every day they would smuggle out tiny quantities of explosive, hidden in match-boxes concealed in small pockets stitched into the hems of their dresses. These they passed on to Rosa, who was the first link in an elaborate chain of communication that led ultimately to a Russian prisoner named Borodin, who was an expert at making bombs. Using empty cans as bomb casings Borodin managed to build up a sizeable stockpile of explosives, which were then distributed to different hiding-places all over the camp complex.

One of the biggest caches of explosives was near the crematorium, and the canisters found their way there hidden in carts that were loaded with corpses. The task of disposing of these bodies fell to a *Sonderkommando* – Special Commando – composed of Jewish prisoners, and it was these unfortunates who planned to lead the uprising. Before their plans were fully complete, however, the members of the *Sonder-kommando* learned that they, too, were about to be liquidated by the Germans. On 7 October, with no hope now of co-ordinating their plans with other resistance groups in the camp, they decided to act. That afternoon they blew up No. 3 crematorium, threw an SS overseer into the flames, shot dead four more SS men and wounded several others. Before the Germans could muster reinforcements the rebels cut their way through the barbed wire fence and about 600 escaped into the surrounding countryside, leaving a handful of their colleagues to sacrifice themselves in an attempt to hold off the renewed attacks of the guards.

A few – very few – of the escapees got away across country and succeeded in joining up with the advancing Russian forces. The remainder were tracked down ruthlessly by police and an SS battalion; 430 were captured alive, dragged back to the camp and shot.

So ended the only armed revolt ever to take place in Auschwitz. After the last revolver shot had died away and the last bloodstained corpse had tumbled face down into its communal grave, the SS began a full investigation with the object of breaking the underground movement for good. In particular they were determined to find out how the explosives had been brought into the camp and how they had been distributed. They arrested several girls from the munitions factory and subjected them to various tortures in the infamous Block 11, where Auschwitz 'interrogations' were carried out – then, amazingly, after a couple of days they let them go.

The rest of the inmates breathed a sigh of relief – but it was destined to be short lived. Within twenty-four hours mass-arrests began of everyone suspected of being implicated in the underground movement. Several hundred people were taken in groups into the surrounding forest and shot.

Rosa Robota was arrested, together with three of the girls who had smuggled explosives out of the factory. Every day they were taken to Block 11 for questioning, and every night they emerged with their faces swollen and bruised beyond recognition, their clothes in rags and their finger ends bloody, stumps where nails had been torn away. Rosa's feet were broken and at the end of each interrogation session she was flung into the compound by two guards, who returned a few hours later to drag her back again. Finally she was imprisoned in the death cell.

Some of her friends in the underground movement took incredible risks to visit her, bribing her SS guard with a bottle of whisky. One of them later described the horror of the death cell:

I had the privilege to see Rosa for the last time several days before her execution. At night, when all the prisoners were asleep and all movement in camp was forbidden, I descended into a bunker of Block 11 and saw the cells and dark corridors. I heard the moaning of the condemned and was shaken to the core of my being. Jacob led me through the stairs to Rosa's cell. He opened the door and let me in. Then he closed the door behind me and disappeared.

When I became accustomed to the dark I noticed a figure, wrapped in torn clothing, lying on the cold cement floor. She turned her head towards me. I hardly recognized her. After several minutes of silence she began to speak. She told me of the sadistic methods the Germans employ during interrogations. It is impossible for a human being to endure them. She told me that she took all the blame upon herself and that she would be the last to go. She had betrayed no one.

I tried to console her but she would not listen. I know what I have done, and what I have to expect, she said.

She asked that the comrades continue with their work. It is easier to die when one knows that the work is being carried on.

I heard the door squeak. Jacob ordered me to come out. We took leave of each other. It was the last time that I saw her.

The Germans executed Rosa and the three other girls by hanging four days later, before the assembled prisoners. The latter stared ahead of them like statues as the sentence was carried out, remembering the simple message that Rosa had smuggled out of her condemned cell only hours before her death.

It said, in Hebrew: '*Khazak V'Hamatz* – Be Strong and Brave'. It was a message that was to strengthen the hearts of many and carry them through to the end of their ordeal, one day to stand as accusers against those who had murdered Rosa Robota and the countless thousands like her.

6 Escape Line

DURING WORLD WAR TWO, Madame Anne Brusselmans helped no fewer than 176 Allied airmen to escape from Brussels. She knew that discovery by the Germans would in all probability mean death, not only for herself but for her whole family, yet she continued with her work until the Liberation.

This is the story of a very brave woman – an ordinary housewife whose determination stemmed, in no small part, from a great affection for the young men who were fighting her country's battle.

One day in September 1943 a Spitfire of no. 302 Squadron – an all-Polish unit forming part of RAF Fighter Command – was crippled by German fighters while carrying out an offensive 'sweep' over Belgium. Its pilot, Flying Officer Bronek Malinowski, although severely wounded in his right leg, made a successful forced landing in a field near Ypres. Scrambling from the wreck, he burrowed under cover among some trees and spent the night there, shivering with cold and pain, while German troops searched for him.

The next morning Malinowski was found by a Belgian workman, who brought him food and cigarettes. The man returned later that day, with a younger man who helped the injured pilot to a nearby farmhouse. From there he was taken to a hospital, where a doctor operated on his leg in secret and nuns nursed him until he was sufficiently recovered to travel further. Eventually the Belgian underground movement smuggled him into Brussels, where he was hidden for several days in a flat in the Chaussée d'Ixelles, one of the city's main thoroughfares. There he was looked after by a quiet young Belgian housewife who seemed quite unperturbed by the constant stream of human traffic – Belgian resistance workers and Allied airmen on the run – that passed through her home.

Her name was Madame Anne Brusselmans. It was a name that was to be remembered for ever with affection and gratitude by the 176 Allied airmen she helped to escape during World War Two, daily running the risk of death for herself, her husband and their two small children.

Anne's involvement with the Belgian Resistance began un-
expectedly in the Autumn of 1941, when she was visited by
her local priest, Pastor Schyns. After a few minutes of polite
conversation, the talk turned to the RAF's mounting bomber
offensive against Germany's cities – and to the growing number
of aircrew who were parachuting from their crippled aircraft
over Belgian territory. Suddenly the pastor took a deep breath
and asked point blank if Anne would be prepared to hide
airmen in her home until they could be smuggled out of the
country. Grimly he pointed out the danger involved – that
if she were caught, her whole family would be tortured and
shot.

Despite the risk Anne agreed to help. She had an English
mother, and therefore her ties with Britain were strong; she
felt it her duty to help the Islanders in their struggle against
the Nazi tyranny.

A few days later the pastor returned, accompanied by
Major Giersé, a retired Belgian Army officer who was responsible for finding 'billets' for the escaping airmen and who
now made a thorough survey of Anne's flat to assess its
security. The following week, Giersé again called at the
Brusselmans' home. With him was a young, ginger-haired man
dressed in the overalls of a Belgian workman – a disguise that
failed to hide the fact that he was unmistakably English. He
was, in fact, an RAF sergeant named Jack Hutton, who had
been shot down several days earlier. He was the first of Anne's
'guests' and he stayed for a fortnight before leaving on the
next lap of his journey home. The flat seemed strangely quiet
after his departure, for the young airman had become a firm
favourite with Anne's children, Jacques and Yvonne, who
had been told that he was a cousin from Antwerp who spoke
only English and Flemish. Since Anne had brought her children up to speak English fluently, they and Jack had no difficulty in conversing.

With Jack's departure, too, something new entered the Brusselmans' lives : a stomach-churning fear every time the doorbell rang. The fear intensified when one day Major Giersé arrived at the flat with his niece, Mary, whose husband had just been arrested by the Gestapo. The Major told Anne that the Germans had raided his house and tried to arrest him, but he had managed to get away. Now he was forced to leave Brussels, at least for the time being, and asked Anne if she would look after Mary until the hue and cry died away. She agreed readily, even though she was then sheltering another airman, a Canadian named John Ives. He stayed with her until the beginning of December 1941 – a week before the Japanese attacked Pearl Harbour. When Anne heard that news she knew that it would be only a matter of time before American airmen joined the RAF boys who were passing through the hands of the Belgian Resistance in a steady stream.

That, however, was still several months away. Meanwhile growing numbers of the RAF's new heavy bombers were pounding the Ruhr Valley. Early in 1942 Anne sheltered her first pair of fugitive Polish airmen, whom she knew simply as Edward and John; both got safely away down the escape line, despite the fact that the Gestapo were then carrying out the first of their large-scale search operations designed to break the nucleus of the Resistance movement in Brussels. By the middle of 1942 the escape route – which ran from Belgium through Paris and over the Pyrenees into Spain – was working so efficiently that Allied airmen were being spirited away from Brussels almost as soon as they arrived.

Nevertheless the Gestapo were enjoying growing success in their campaign against the Belgian underground. One day Anne telephoned the home of a resistance colleague, but it was the Gestapo who answered the phone. For long minutes, Anne was paralysed with fear; her first instinct was to run away before the Gestapo came, to take her children and flee from the Nazi torturers. Then reason took hold of her, and she knew that she could do nothing but wait and see what happened. There was nowhere else to go. That evening she went through the flat from end to end, turning out drawers in a desperate search for any incriminating evidence that might have been accidentally left behind by her airmen. Then she sat down to wait out the long hours of the night, reasoning that if the Gestapo came, it would be at dawn.

Some time later she was awakened from a fitful doze by a hand on her shoulder. It was daylight, and the hand belonged not to some German thug but to her husband, Julien, who had brought her a hot drink. She wept with relief.

As the New Year of 1943 dawned the oppressed in Belgium and the other occupied countries took fresh heart from the growing number of reverses being inflicted on the Germans. In North Africa the remnants of the German forces were being hounded to destruction in Tunisia; in Russia the Sixth Army was fighting its last battle in Stalingrad; and in the Atlantic the Allies were at last beginning to beat the U-boat menace. For the people of Brussels war meant the drone of bombers, passing overhead nightly towards their targets in the Third Reich; constant food shortages, accompanied by outrageous prices on the black market; field-grey uniforms everywhere – and the sinister men of the Gestapo in their leather overcoats, with their equally sinister headquarters in the Avenue Louise.

For Anne and her resistance colleagues that house in the Avenue Louise was the focal point of all hatred. There, on file, were the details behind the deportation and death of people whom she had known personally, and behind the arrest and interrogation of countless more. How, in those dark winter days of 1942-3, she wished that someone, somehow, might strike at the Gestapo snake in its lair!

The wish was realized on 20 January 1943, a day on which

the inhabitants of Brussels went wild with delight. Appropriately enough, the man responsible was a son of an old and noble Belgian family : his name was Flight Lieutenant Baron Jean de Selys Longchamps. He had escaped from Dunkirk in 1940, joined the RAF and now flew with no. 609 Squadron – the first unit to be equipped with the new and deadly Hawker Typhoon fighters.

The events of that January day were described by Frank Zeigler, 609 Squadron's intelligence officer : 'For weeks I had been trying to get permission from 11 Group for Jean to carry out a cherished idea : a single-handed attack on the Gestapo headquarters in the heart of Brussels. He had it all worked out, but Group had postponed their consent, and this morning he had taken off with a fellow countryman on a normal "Rhubarb", but with a cockpit full of flags.' Jean crossed the Channel, flying very low, and roared over the Belgian coast. He shot up a couple of trains, zoomed over the rooftops of Ghent, then turned east towards Brussels.

He had never seen his native Brussels from the air before, and must have felt like a winged angel of revenge as his lone Typhoon almost brushed the Cinquantenaire memorial and his old cavalry barracks. Close to the target lay the familiar Palais de Justice. Justice indeed! A rebellious instinct made him press the button of his camera gun. Now to the task. Boulevard de Waterloo, Porte Louise, Avenue Louise. There it was stretching to the south-east, almost two miles in length, with that hated building at the end. No flak as yet, but he mustn't make a mess of it – mustn't kill any Belgians, must riddle all those windows behind which the Gestapo was weaving its deadly web.

Anne Brusselmans was hanging out her washing when Jean's Typhoon passed overhead, so low that it blotted out the sun and sent her radio aerial tumbling into the yard with its slipstream. Seconds later she heard the thump of its cannon, then caught sight of it again as it zoomed up in a steep climb. Almost immediately sirens began to wail as German ambulances raced towards the Gestapo headquarters, through the big double bay windows of which Jean had sent a stream of cannon shells with great accuracy.

The pilot had not finished yet. Coming out of his climb, he looked down and saw a square crowded with people, their faces upturned. Sliding back his cockpit canopy, he pushed out a large Union Jack and a Belgian flag, followed by handfuls of miniature flags, before turning towards the coast. Thirty minutes later he was back in England and making his report.

Jean's exploit earned him a Distinguished Flying Cross – and a temporary loss of rank. For although his shells had killed and wounded thirty Gestapo men, it turned out that one of them had been a British agent who would prove impossible to replace.

Nevertheless the attack made Jean a legend throughout Belgium and boosted the determination of the whole resistance movement. It also made the Germans more savagely determined to break the back of the resistance, and in the spring of 1943 their chance came when one of the network's most trusted couriers turned out to be a double agent. In one huge swoop the Germans struck at key points of the escape line from Brussels to Paris and arrested over a hundred people, all of them vital to the operation. The escape line had collapsed, but the flow of Allied airmen reaching Brussels continued and something had to be done to evacuate them. Anne realized that everything would have to begin all over again, right from scratch. The problem was that she had no idea how many contacts – if any – along the old escape route had managed to avoid arrest when the Germans pounced. In Brussels itself several people who had sheltered airmen over the past months had also been arrested, which meant that new accommodation had to be found for the fugitives who at that moment were waiting to be smuggled into the city.

Anne took it upon herself to make the necessary moves, although a fearsome risk was involved. It was not just a matter of approaching old friends and asking them politely if they would help; loyalties had changed during the bitter years of the occupation, and a former trusted friend might now turn out to be a collaborator. Most of the peasants in the surrounding villages were loyal to the last, but in the city itself it was a different story. The Germans were offering 10,000 francs for every Allied airman turned over to them – a powerful incentive to people living perilously close to starvation level, and especially those with children to feed.

Nevertheless Anne succeeded in recruiting a new pool of helpers, and the stream of fugitive airmen began to flow again. Anne's task was doubly exhausting, for it was her responsibility to screen the British and American airmen who passed through Brussels, and this had to be carried out with complete thoroughness. The shock of the recent mass-arrests was still too fresh in the Belgians' minds for them to take any chances, especially as it was known that the Germans were trying to infiltrate agents dressed in RAF uniforms into the escape line. On one occasion Anne's feminine intuition saved her from arrest when, for no reason she could put her finger on, she became suspicious of an airman she was supposed to meet near the Palais de Justice. At the last moment she decided not to keep the rendezvous. It was just as well: the 'airman' failed to turn up, but the Gestapo did.

Although her work with the fugitives kept her occupied day and night, she nevertheless found time to help the Allied cause in other ways as the opportunity arose. She noticed, for example, that most of the airmen reaching Brussels had been shot down by flak in the Westerloo area, which seemed to indicate that the defences there were particularly strong. She determined to find out more about them and caught a train for Westerloo, booking herself into a hotel – which, incidentally, was full of German soldiers.

That night the RAF were over in strength. Anne stood at the window of her room, watching the German searchlights and anti-aircraft fire. With the aid of a tiny compass – part of an airman's escape kit – she pinpointed the direction from which the most intense fire seemed to be coming: the north-west.

The next morning she took a stroll towards the direction the firing had come from. In a field on the outskirts of the town she located the camouflaged gun emplacements. That same night she returned to Brussels, and in the privacy of her flat she prepared a sketch-map of what she had seen. Within forty-eight hours the map – together with Anne's detailed report – was on its way to London.

In Brussels airmen were being spirited out of Belgium at the rate of ten a week. Sometimes Anne had to meet and interrogate as many as four a day and find them safe lodgings in the city. Meanwhile the Gestapo squeeze was tightening steadily, and more of Anne's colleagues were arrested. She herself seemed to bear a charmed life; on more than one occasion in the course of her work she visited a contact only to find that the Gestapo had pounced on him only minutes earlier. Then, early in 1944, came another blow: a resistance worker broke down under Gestapo torture and revealed the addresses of several vital 'clearing houses' where fugitive airmen were sheltered. Anne's was not among them, but almost all her contacts were arrested; it was virtually a clean sweep. Once again she was on her own, faced with the prospect of getting the waiting airmen out of Brussels single handed.

This time the task of reorganizing the escape line was

formidable. Anne received news that the Paris end of it was still intact, but it was almost impossible to find guides who were willing to take the airmen from, Brussels to the French capital.

Meanwhile the weeks passed – and Brussels became so full of airmen that if the Gestapo decided to launch a full-scale house-to-house search it would end in disaster for the Belgian Resistance. The fugitives were sure to be discovered and the result would be the taking of hostages, more mass-arrests, more torture, more executions.

The strain that had to be endured by all concerned was almost unbearable. It was one thing to ask a Belgian to shelter a fugitive airman for a day or two; quite another to ask for refuge to be provided for several weeks. The airmen themselves were perhaps more nervous than anyone else; apart from the fact that they had been shuttled round from one hiding-place to another for much longer than they had expected, there were strong rumours that the Allies were about to launch an invasion of Europe and the men wanted to get back home to play their part in it.

In April 1944 there were forty-nine airmen in Brussels, and only a handful were getting away to Paris. Some of the delay had been caused by the Allies themselves, because they had recently bombed the railway junction at Charleville and it now took three days to reach the French capital, instead of only a few hours. In May, to make matters worse, the Allies struck at rail targets in Brussels itself, and it was inevitable that a great many homes should be destroyed. The result was that a number of Belgians became hostile towards the airmen they knew to be sheltering in their midst; it was a dangerous and explosive situation.

By this time the Germans knew that a woman was responsible for the Brussels end of the escape line, although as yet they did not know her identity. Towards the end of May

three of her closest contacts were arrested and she knew that
the net round her was tightening – that her liberty, perhaps
even life itself, was measured in days.

Then, on 6 June 1944, the oppressed millions of occupied
Europe tuned in to the BBC on their clandestine radios and
heard the news that sent them wild with elation : Allied forces
had landed in Normandy. Anne Brusselmans was among the
countless ordinary people who wept with joy that night.

It now became a question not so much of getting the airmen
away, but of keeping them safely hidden in Brussels until the
Allies arrived. With the news of the Allied invasion, the
attitude of the citizens of Brussels changed almost overnight;
people who had previously been reluctant to help now became
overwhelmingly eager to show their loyalty by hiding the fugitives – including at least one collaborator who feared retribu-
tion when the Allies came.

Hiding the airmen for a lengthy period, however, gave rise
to the problem of feeding them in a city that was almost
starving. Anne and her colleagues received invaluable help
in this respect from members of the White Army, the armed
section of the Belgian Resistance who had been stockpiling
supplies and arms against the day when they could come out
into the streets and fight as the Allies approached. Whenever
the White Army carried out a raid on a German food convoy
some of the supplies found their way to the escape line. The
White Army helped in other ways, too; on one occasion its
agents tracked down a collaborator who had been spying on
Anne and executed him before he could pass on his information to the Gestapo.

The progress of the Allies was slower than had been expected, and all the time more airmen arrived in the city. They
all had to be provided with accommodation, food and clothing, and for Anne and her fellow workers this was the most
hectic time of all. One of the most difficult tasks of all was

to persuade the airmen to stay where they were; at least one joined the White Army and was killed outside Brussels in a skirmish.

In August the city was in ferment as the news came that the Allies had liberated Paris. By the end of the month the British were in Amiens, and on 2 September Montgomery's Second Army was across the Belgian frontier and heading rapidly for the capital. The Germans were pulling out of Brussels now in a steady stream – but for the gallant men and women of the Resistance, the danger was not yet over.

At about 11 o'clock in the evening of 3 September Anne and her husband were startled by a knock at their door. It was the German police, armed to the teeth with sub-machine-guns. They burst in and began to search the flat, pulling apart one room after another until they came to the bedroom normally occupied by Anne's son, Jacques. With his hand on the door handle, one of the Germans paused and asked Anne what was inside. Taking a deep breath, she told him that the room contained only her son – who was suffering from typhoid fever. The German let go of the door handle as though it was red-hot and left hurriedly, together with his colleagues.

Anne almost collapsed with relief. Inside Jacques's room was a young resistance worker, on his way to join the secret army of the resistance. If the Germans had found him, it would have spelled death for all of them.

Two days later, just after 6 pm on 5 September, Anne was brought to the window of her flat by the sound of wild cheering in the streets. Looking down, she saw a crowd thronging round a motorcycle. Its rider wore a steel helmet, perched on the back of his head, and he was unmistakably British.

The next morning Anne went to the Hôtel Metropole, where she heard that the British had set up their headquarters. Reporting to an astonished young lieutenant, she stated bluntly that there were fifty-four Allied airmen in

Brussels; she wanted to know what to do with them. 'Well,' said the officer, 'I suppose you'd better bring them here.'

So from all over Brussels the airmen converged on the Hôtel Metropole. On the morning of 9 September a convoy of trucks arrived to take them to Paris, from where they were to be flown to Britain.

Anne watched them go. They waved to her and sang 'For she's a jolly good fellow' as they drove away. She held her two children close to her and watched until the trucks passed from view, tears streaming down her face. And as she watched, she overheard a whispered comment from someone close by in the crowd : 'Look at her. Anyone would think she was losing her children.'

7 Nancy Wake - Resistance Leader

THE STORY OF THE resistance heroines of World War Two is legendary. For five long years, over the length and breadth of Nazi-occupied Europe, they risked death and torture to play their part in the struggle for freedom. This is the story of one of them – an Australian girl who gave up everything to fight for her adopted country, sten-gun in hand, personally leading several thousand tough guerrillas in the long battle against Germany's picked SS troops.

For Nancy Wake that summer of 1939 was as near perfect as any summer could possibly be. She had everything a woman could wish for; a full social life, plenty of money, a rich fiancé and a beautiful home into which they would move when they married in a few weeks' time. She was twenty-three years old and her fiancé, Henri Fiocca, a steel industrialist, was fourteen years older. He had met her at a party in Cannes and had at once been captivated by this beautiful Australian girl who had decided to leave her homeland and embark on a world tour, supporting herself by freelance journalism. Her travels had brought her to Paris, where she managed to earn enough to support herself and keep on moving round France, a country that she grew to love.

After a whirlwind courtship Nancy and Fiocca became engaged. They were to marry in November 1939 and move into a luxury apartment in Marseilles. Yet in the midst of her idyll Nancy knew that the storm clouds were gathering over Europe. She knew with a terrible certainty that war was coming, and soon. At the outbreak of hostilities Henri was certain to be called up for service with the French Army, and when that happened she too was determined to play her part.

In August 1939 she went to Britain for three weeks; she was still there on 3 September when war broke out, and immediately offered her services to the British. All the British authorities could suggest, however, was that she might be able to work in a NAAFI canteen. She politely but firmly declined and returned to France.

She and Henri were married on 30 November 1939. A few
weeks later Henri was called up. Nancy, far from content to
sit in Marseilles for the duration of the war, embarked on a
crash driving course, which she completed in a single day,
and afterwards volunteered to become an ambulance driver.
During the months that followed she worked in northern
France, helping to evacuate refugees from the threatened
frontier zones and carrying truck-loads of clothing to the
refugee centres. She was still engaged in this work when the
Germans attacked on 10 May 1940 and the whole French
military structure in the north began to break down into
complete chaos.

For Nancy the next few weeks were a nightmare. Day after
day she forced her ambulance along the congested roads of
northern France and Belgium, battling her way through
streams of terrified refugees and weaponless troops fleeing
from the front before the relentless advance of the German
armoured divisions. The sight of blood had always been repug-
nant to her and now she was sickened by what she saw – corpses
strewn along the roadsides, helpless civilians machine-gunned
by German fighters. For two weeks she hardly slept as she
drove her ambulance on a ferry service between the front
and the makeshift dressing stations to the rear, laden with
blood-stained cargoes of Allied troops. On 28 May the Belgians
capitulated. Nancy filled her ambulance with one last load
of injured men and drove southwards to French territory.
There was no longer any semblance of organization. After
the defeat of Belgium she simply did what she could wherever
she could, carrying civilians as well as soldiers away from the
thunder of guns in the north.

On 13 June she was in Paris, sleeping an exhausted sleep,
when the Germans reached the capital. Despite her tiredness
she at once climbed into her ambulance and drove southwards,
eager to reach Marseilles before she fell into the German

trap. A few miles outside Paris her ambulance broke down and she completed the rest of the journey by hitch-hiking. Immediately on her return she went to her father-in-law's house and asked if there was news of Henri. There was none. This, on top of the terrible sights she had witnessed over the past few weeks, almost broke her spirit. For two days she stayed in her room and wept. She remained inconsolable until that wonderful day three weeks later when Henri at last came home.

The Armistice had been signed, and they were fortunate in that they lived in that part of France that was as yet free from German domination; but life in Vichy France, although retaining some semblance of normality, was constantly over-shadowed by a cloud of fear, for the inhabitants knew that at any moment the Germans could occupy the whole of their country to the Mediterranean coast if the situation demanded it. In this atmosphere of tension the Vichy government collaborated openly with the Germans, and southern France was riddled with German agents who openly pulled the strings of the Milice, Vichy's own police force, who could be every bit as deadly and brutal as the Gestapo.

Nevertheless by September 1940 – while the Battle of Britain was being fought and won on the other side of the Channel – Henri and Nancy had managed to pick up most of the threads of their life, a process that was made easier by Henri's wealth. Unlike many other people of position in France at this time, however, they made no attempt to hoard their possessions. Instead they were generous to a fault, freely distributing what they had among their less fortunate friends and acquaintances.

Although to some extent isolated from direct contact with the war, Nancy was desperately anxious to help with the Allied effort. Her opportunity to do so came almost by accident. One night, while sitting in a Marseilles bar waiting for

D

Henri, she noticed a tall, fair-haired man at a nearby table, quietly reading a book. With something of a shock she noticed too that the book he was reading was English. At first Nancy thought that the man must be a German spy; no one else would be foolish enough to sit in a Marseilles bar reading an English book. A few minutes later Henri arrived and Nancy explained her suspicions to him. He at once offered to find out who the man really was. In the course of the next few minutes Henri discovered that the man was in fact a British officer, one of many – all of them stragglers from the earlier campaign in the north – who had been rounded up by the Vichy forces and interned at the fortress in Marseilles.

The man explained that the prisoners were frequently let out on parole to wander through the streets of the town. After talking to him at some length, Nancy promised to meet him the following day and hand over to him a thousand cigarettes and a radio on which the prisoners could listen to the BBC. Twenty-four hours later the man turned up on time, bringing with him two friends, also British officers. That night the three dined in Nancy's flat. From then on parties of British officers became frequent visitors to the home of Nancy and Henri. Nancy revelled in it, although a considerable risk was involved. If she made one false step, if the story of her liaison with the British officers leaked out, she would almost certainly be arrested by the Milice.

One of Nancy's British visitors was a Captain Ian Garrow. A tall Scot, Garrow was in the process of organizing an escape route from Vichy France across the Pyrenees to Spain and Gibraltar, and on learning that Nancy was co-operative and keen to help he at once determined to enlist her services. Nancy agreed without hesitation, despite Henri's fears for their safety, and their Marseilles flat soon became the headquarters of the escape organization. Although there was a certain amount of gossip about the number of visitors she was receiving every day, Nancy went out of her way to lead an unpretentious life in Marseilles. Behind the scenes, however, she and Henri were both very active, often leading parties of escaping prisoners to various points on the escape route and delivering mysterious packages to underground agents in Cannes and Toulon. The packages were mostly parts of radio transmitters, all of which were destined to find their way to the various groups of the rapidly expanding French resistance movement.

Such then was the pattern of Nancy's life for the next eighteen months, during which she helped more than a thousand people to escape. As well as internees and escaping prisoners-of-war there were now added to the list a growing number of British airmen who had been shot down during operations over the Continent and who had managed to evade the German search parties and get across the border into Vichy France. To divert suspicion from herself, Nancy assumed the false identity of Mademoiselle Cartier during her clandestine trips across southern France, reverting to her legal status of Nancy Fiocca on her return to Marseilles.

The escape network was still expanding when, in November 1942, disaster struck. The Germans, worried by the Allied successes in North Africa and the possibility of Allied landings on the French Riviera, decided to occupy Vichy France with the three-fold aim of seizing the French fleet that lay in Toulon, fortifying the Mediterranean coast against a possible Allied invasion and operating from the French Mediterranean ports with their motor torpedo boats and submarines. The entry of the Germans into southern France was marked by an upsurge in the activities of the Gestapo, whose primary concern was to smash the various escape organizations that flourished there. Before long German agents were doing everything in their power to track down one of the leaders of the escape network, a mysterious individual known to them by the code name of the 'White Mouse'. Fortunately they were

a long way from suspecting that the 'White Mouse' was none other than the respectable Nancy Fiocca.

As part of their programme to crush the underground movement the Gestapo imposed a system of regular checks on passengers travelling across southern France by train. This made the process of transferring groups of escaping prisoners from one point to another infinitely more hazardous, but more than that the presence of German agents and soldiers in uniform on French trains drove Nancy to cold heights of fury. On one occasion she shared a compartment with a German officer and a little French soldier who was still in uniform. After a while the ticket collector came into the first-class compartment and ordered the French soldier to leave on the grounds that he had only a second-class ticket. The Frenchman protested that all the other seats were full, and that this compartment was virtually empty. The ticket collector, however, remained adamant and began to grow aggressive. At this point Nancy flew into a towering rage. Why, she cried, should Frenchmen who had fought for their country be denied seats on their own trains when Boche officers could sit in comfort? For five minutes she dressed down both the ticket collector and the astonished German officer and ended by paying the balance of the fare for the French soldier. A minute or two later, the discomfited German got up and left the compartment.

By the beginning of 1943 the 'White Mouse' was the object of a full-scale search by teams of Gestapo agents operating in Marseilles, and Nancy's position became increasingly perilous. As time went by she felt sure that she was being watched and confided her fears to Henri; the latter decided that his wife must leave France for Britain, and the sooner the better. A couple of days later she left for Toulouse as a first step on her journey to Gibraltar. While at Toulouse she continued to work for the organization, making frequent trips to Perpignan. As she was returning from one of these expeditions, the train in which she was travelling was suddenly stopped and everyone in it was arrested and bundled into trucks, which set off in convoy for the police headquarters in Toulouse. On its way through the narrow streets Nancy's truck was halted at a crossroads by traffic. She seized her chance, jumped over the tailboard and fled. Unfortunately, she got mixed up with a crowd of students who had been demonstrating elsewhere in the town and who were being hotly pursued by the police. In the ensuing mêlée Nancy was knocked down, and picked herself up to find herself looking into the muzzle of a rifle.

For four days Nancy was interrogated by the police, receiving frequent beatings, when – miraculously – she was rescued by a resistance colleague called Patrick O'Leary, a mysterious Belgian of uncertain background who was one of the underground movement's leading workers. (O'Leary's real name was, in fact, Dr Albert-Marie-Edmond Guerisse. He was later caught by the Gestapo and survived Dachau concentration camp. After the war he was awarded the George Cross. Today, with the rank of major-general, he is the Belgian Army's senior medical officer.) O'Leary produced false papers that declared him to be a member of the Vichy police and stated blandly that he was a personal friend of Laval, puppet dictator of the Vichy regime. The mere mention of Laval was enough; the police let Nancy go.

During the next few weeks Nancy made five unsuccessful attempts to get into Spain, but each time she was foiled by an unexpected swoop on the escape routes by Vichy police and Gestapo agents. It was clear that for the time being at least the Gestapo were winning the battle against the underground, and the carefully planned organization was gradually being broken up. On the sixth attempt she joined a party consisting of O'Leary, two Frenchmen and a New Zealand airman who had been shot down over France, and boarded a train bound for Perpignan on the frontier. As time went by the party began to relax – then, suddenly, the door of the compartment was flung open and a French railway official hissed a warning that the Germans were going to check the train. There was only one thing for it : the party decided to jump. Nancy wormed her way through the window, pushed herself away from the carriage and fell on the track, picking herself up with only a few bruises and running towards a vineyard that flanked the railway line. As she did so a German machine-gun opened up and bullets sliced their way through the branches round her. She ran as she had never run before, not taking the trouble to dodge the fire until she considered she had put sufficient distance between herself and the train, and then, exhausted, she collapsed on the ground and waited apprehensively to see if the others had also been successful in getting away. A few minutes later they joined her, gasping for breath. There was one exception : one of the Frenchmen had been captured. He was later sent to a concentration camp and died there of typhus.

For the next few days Nancy and the others stayed on the run. By this time they were convinced that their escape network had been infiltrated by Gestapo agents and this was confirmed when, while they were in Toulouse, O'Leary was arrested. Taking her life in her hands Nancy returned to Marseilles to warn the other members of the group that it would be only a question of time before the Gestapo pounced. Then, taking a couple of escaping airmen with her, she boarded a train for Nice, where she was sheltered by a courageous Frenchwoman named Madame Sainson, known under the resistance name of Delilah.

She stayed with Madame Sainson for three weeks; then, with a small group of airmen and a local guide, she set off on foot to cross the Pyrenees into Spain. It was a nightmare journey. They had to cross 50 miles of some of the roughest country in the world, which was heavily patrolled by Germans and police. To make matters worse, they were all suffering from mild food poisoning caused by some black-market lamb they had eaten earlier. The trek lasted forty-seven hours, much of it through a raging blizzard that lashed them with razor-edged particles of ice and snow. One of the American airmen in the party collapsed, protesting that he could go no further; it was Nancy who slapped his face until his stupor left him and he felt able to carry on. Finally, half-dead from fatigue, they stumbled across the shallow part of a river. On the other side they halted, hardly daring to comprehend that they were now on Spanish territory.

Nancy reached Britain by sea at the end of June 1943, having sailed from Gibraltar. After resting for a couple of weeks she visited the Free French headquarters in London and volunteered to return to France in some role, possibly that of saboteur. The French proved to be uninterested. At this stage of the war there was considerable antagonism between the Free French headquarters and the British War Office, the French being convinced that the British were spying on their activities. As it turned out the French were probably right in their suspicions, for soon after Nancy's visit she was called on by a War Office representative who suggested that she should apply to join the Special Operations Executive under the command of the famous Colonel Buckmaster. Shortly afterwards Buckmaster himself forestalled Nancy's application by requesting that she should enlist in his group – which she did, but in her maiden name.

The group she joined was known misleadingly by the initials FANY, which stood for First Aid Nursing Yeomanry. The unit had been formed in 1907, legitimately enough, as a first-aid group, primarily to give an opportunity for wealthy upper-class women to serve their country, but during World War Two it became a cover under which women volunteers trained as saboteurs and resistance organizers for infiltration into occupied countries. Nancy, newly appointed to the rank of ensign, soon found herself plunged into a tough training course that included all aspects of the trade of spy and saboteur, including demolition, the science of making one's own explosives from ingredients that could be bought at any chemist's shop, weapons practice with a wide variety of small arms from revolvers to Sten guns, the art of silent killing with a knife or bare hands, radio operation and the use of map and compass.

She was by no means a natural student, and her antics during the training course often had her male companions reduced to helpless fits of laughter. There was the time, for example, when she decided to go through the middle of a car tyre that formed part of an obstacle course, rather than over or under it, and lost her trousers in the process. She finished the course in her underclothes, accompanied by howls of mirth from her team mates. On another occasion an instructor explained to her at great length how to pull the pin from a grenade and throw it. Nancy, whose mind had been wandering and who had not heard a word, suddenly asked him what she had to do. Exasperated, the instructor said with heavy sarcasm, 'Pull the pin, throw the grenade into the trench and run.' With a deadpan face, Nancy pretended to carry out his instructions to the letter and the class in the trench, which included the instructor, were last seen running for cover while Nancy doubled up with laughter behind them. For much of the course she cheated unashamedly, taking short cuts on cross-country runs, skipping PT practice on the pretence of having a cold and circumventing obstacle courses with an ingenuity that earned her full marks for initiative.

Despite everything, she finally completed the course early in 1944 and was declared a fully operational agent. All that remained for her now was to be kitted out as a Frenchwoman, provided with forged papers and a cover story and parachuted into France. She was given the code name of Hélène for use by London and Madame Andrée for use by the Resistance. She was also required to assist the War Office's cryptographers in forming a personal code that would form the basis of messages passed to her over the radio. Most agents chose a verse from the Bible or Shakespeare or a favourite book to provide the necessary ingredients for such a code; typically, Nancy chose a rude rhyme.

Finally, on the night of 29 February 1944, all was ready. Together with another agent named Hubert she was taken to an airfield in southern England and there she boarded a Liberator special duties aircraft that was to fly her to occupied France. The drop took place over Montlucon and was fault-less. She and Hubert quickly made contact with local resist-ance workers who were at the dropping zone to meet them, and were soon being whisked off through the pitch darkness to a safe hiding-place. Their area of operations was in the province of Auverne, a highland district which seemed to be ready made for guerrilla warfare. With mountains as high as 6000 feet, intermingled with plateaux, gorges, rugged rock formations and densely wooded slopes, together with a climate that was cold and wet for most of the year, it was virtually inaccessible and guerrilla bands could simply melt away among its natural ruggedness.

Nancy set up her headquarters at Chaudes-Aigues, where she found herself in command of more than 7000 men. They represented in fact the whole of the Maquis of the Auvergne, who had been without a leader since their last one had been killed in a German raid. Her first task was to call the leaders of the various groups together to brief them on future opera-tions. It was no easy task, for they were a tough, hard-bitten crowd who resented being given orders by a woman. They soon discovered, however, that she was a match for them in almost every respect, including the ability to drink and swear, and it was not long before she began to earn their admiration.

The life of a *maquisard* in Auvergne was tough and danger-ous, for this was one of the strongholds of the French Resist-ance and the Germans went to great lengths to stamp it out. The population suffered heavily, for by way of reprisals the Germans often burned down farmhouses and murdered their inhabitants as well as taking hostages, who were almost invari-ably executed. On 20 June 1944 a pitched battle developed when 22,000 SS troops supported by aircraft and artillery launched a full-scale attack on the stronghold at Chaudes-Aigues. During the height of the battle Nancy worked cease-lessly, distributing truck-loads of weapons, ammunition and supplies to the Maquis outposts. Most of these journeys were made under heavy fire, and on one occasion she had a narrow escape when the farmhouse in which she was snatching a few minutes' rest was hit by a shell. She had a second brush with death that same evening: as she was taking urgent orders to the leader of one of the resistance groups, two German aircraft dived down and machine-gunned her car, riddling it with bullets that all miraculously missed her.

For five minutes the planes followed her as she zigzagged along a treacherous mountain road. Finally another burst of gunfire immobilized her vehicle and she was forced to take shelter in a ditch. A second later the car exploded. Conscious that every second was vital, Nancy and the vehicle's other occupant, a young member of the Resistance, completed their journey on foot, alternately running for their lives and shelter-ing in a ditch as the aircraft dived and strafed time after time. At last the aircraft flew away, probably short of fuel or ammu-nition, leaving the two unharmed except for a severe shaking.

Fifteen hundred German troops died during the fierce fighting that day, but the Resistance suffered heavily too, and Nancy and the survivors were forced to slip away under cover of darkness. In July 1944 she set up a new headquarters in the Allier district, where she commanded a force of 2000 *maquisards* together with a resistance leader named Tardivat. By this time Allied forces were firmly established on the Normandy beach-heads and the main function of Nancy's resistance groups was to ambush German convoys that were moving up supplies and reinforcements to the Normandy front. It was dangerous and exciting work, depending wholly on surprise and fast action. The tactics were simple. A resistance group would lie in wait by the side of a road and as the German convoy rolled past they would wreck the first and last vehicles, bringing the remainder to a halt. Then the resistance men would hurl their grenades and petrol bombs, open up furiously with their small arms for a minute and then melt away into the woods. These raids continued throughout August and culminated in the seizure of a synthetic oil plant at Saint-Hilaire. From then on the Maquis, most of whose cars up to now had been run on charcoal, had all the petrol they needed and, at the same time, a potential source of fuel was denied to the Germans.

In August 1944 the Allies also came ashore in southern France, and before long the German armies in the south, their reserves denuded to meet the demands of the Normandy front, were in full retreat towards the German border. It was at the start of this retreat that the Germans made one last attempt to destroy the resistance headquarters; they mounted an attack with 6000 men against a position held by 200 of Nancy's *maquisards*. Nancy, having been warned that the Germans were coming up the road supported by armoured cars, took twenty men and two American officers who had recently been parachuted to join her, and prepared an ambush. As the first armoured cars came in sight the Americans opened up with a bazooka and knocked them out one after the other. Nancy and the others held on at the cost of some casualties, firing with machine-guns until more resistance men led by Tardivat attacked the German flank. The enemy, believing that they were being attacked by a far superior force, retreated.

During all this time the Gestapo were still active, continuing their reign of terror among the French towns and villages. It was during a reprisal against these actions that Nancy took part in what was probably the most dangerous mission of her career. Together with Tardivat and fourteen others she attacked the Gestapo headquarters in Montlucon, dashing into the building and raking the rooms with small arms fire and grenades and killing thirty-eight Germans. She and the Frenchmen got clean away, despite the fact that the town was full of German troops.

Nancy, who had by this time been promoted to captain, now went into action wearing full military battledress complete with badges of rank. The *maquisards* too wore military uniforms of one sort or another, and during the last week in August, when they attacked Montlucon and drove out the Germans, the whole populace turned out in the streets, cheering enthusiastically in the belief that the first Allied troops had arrived. As it happened the *maquisards'* stay in Montlucon was short lived, for shortly afterwards the Germans sent in an overwhelmingly strong force that counter-attacked. Unable to hold on, Nancy and her men were compelled to retreat into the forest once more.

Later Nancy admitted that she thoroughly enjoyed the danger and excitement of her work. There was, however, one exception. One night she formed part of a force that went out to raid a factory making machine tools for the Germans. Along with several others, her task was to put the German sentries out of action. She crept up to her particular victim, who had his back to her, intending to dispose of him with a blow to the head. At the last moment however he turned to face her, and it was now that her training in unarmed combat saved her life. Before the man had a chance to react she leapt on him and broke his neck with one single swift stroke. It was the only time that she was ever called upon to kill anyone with her bare hands, and the incident left her severely shaken.

Soon after this, in September 1944, Allied troops liberated Nancy's area of operation and her dangerous war was over. It was only now that personal tragedy came home to her. In the middle of September she learned that her husband Henri had been arrested and tortured by the Gestapo, who finally executed him on 16 October 1943. Throughout the whole of his imprisonment he had stubbornly refused to reveal the whereabouts of his wife, even under the most fearful torture. For a time the news left her desolate, but her months of service with the Maquis and the horrors she had witnessed had made her resilient and it was not long before she began to pick up the threads of her life once more.

Now came the acclaim and the awards. France awarded her two Croix de Guerre with Palms, a third Croix de Guerre with Star and a Resistance Medal. From America came the Medal of Freedom with Bronze Palm and from Britain the George Medal – a surprising award, for others had received the George Cross, a much higher decoration, for far less achievement.

Nevertheless she was content. She had fought for and helped to liberate the people she had grown to love, and had contributed more to that battle for freedom than she would ever have dreamed possible just four short years earlier. So ended the story of Nancy Wake, freedom fighter by accident and one of the bravest of them all.

8 The Martyrs

DURING WORLD WAR TWO three incredibly courageous women were awarded the George Cross for their work with the French Resistance. Two of them died; one, miraculously, survived. These are their stories.

VIOLETTE

On 17 December 1946, the *London Gazette* announced the posthumous award of the George Cross to Madame Violette Szabo. The citation was as follows:

Madame Szabo volunteered for a particularly dangerous mission in France in April 1944 and undertook the task with enthusiasm. In her execution of the delicate researches entailed she showed a great presence of mind and astuteness. She was twice arrested by the German security authorities but each time managed to get away. Eventually, however, with other members of her group, she was surrounded in a house in the south west of France. Resistance appeared hopeless, but Madame Szabo, seizing a Sten gun and as much ammunition as she could carry, barricaded herself in part of the house, and exchanging shot for shot with the enemy killed or wounded several of them. By constant movement she avoided being cornered and fought until she dropped exhausted.* She was arrested and had to undergo solitary confinement. She was then continuously and atrociously tortured but never by word or deed gave anything of any value. She was ultimately executed. Madame Szabo gave a magnificent example of courage and steadfastness.

Such was the epitaph of one of the bravest women in history. The child of a British father and French mother who had met
_____
* The account of her capture was later modified when the full story became known.

and married in World War One, it was not unnatural that she should owe deep patriotic allegiance to both countries, and in the Autumn of 1941, at the age of twenty, she offered her services to the ATS with a spirit of determination to play her part in the stand of the British people against the powers of darkness. Her young husband, Etienne Szabo, was a soldier in the French Foreign Legion, which formed part of the Free French Forces under General Charles de Gaulle. They were happy during the all too brief time they had together, and in October 1942 tragedy engulfed Violette's life with the news that Etienne had been killed in action in North Africa.

His death left her completely alone at the age of twenty-two with a four-month-old daughter, Tania, whom Etienne had never seen. Her bitterness and hatred for the Germans were immeasurable. All she wanted now was to play a more active part in the war, and since she spoke fluent French it was natural that she should ultimately find her way to the highly secret corridors of the Special Operations Executive in the War Office, where she was interviewed for the first time in the Spring of 1943. Her training as a secret agent began in the Autumn of that year and she plunged into the strenuous course enthusiastically, astonishing both her colleagues and instructors alike by her prowess. Not only was her French excellent but she proved to be a born athlete and remarkably good shot, as well as possessing a spirit of adventure coupled with a more than usually high degree of intelligence. Moreover her early bereavement had made her mature, and she sensed that she had to complete the training-course with high marks if she was to have an early chance of being sent on operations.

This goal she achieved easily, and in April 1944 she was infiltrated into France to act as courier for a Frenchman whose resistance circuit, which was based at Rouen, had been broken up by the Gestapo, and who was now returning to France in an attempt to re-form an underground group in this area, which was of high strategic importance in the forthcoming Allied invasion plans. Since the Germans were still vigilant and it was not safe for the Frenchman to be seen in Rouen, it was Violette's job to travel there from Paris on her own to try to contact a number of people who had belonged to the former underground circuit and who were believed to have escaped the clutches of the Nazis. It was a highly dangerous task, for Rouen was in a military area that encompassed the Channel ports and was consequently under special restrictions. Nevertheless Violette succeeded in making her contacts and was able to provide her chief with a complete assessment of the situation. She also brought back with her a German 'Wanted' poster torn from a wall in the streets of Rouen, bearing a photograph of her leader and his wireless operator and their descriptions as they appeared on their forged identity papers. This document was of considerable value as it revealed that the Gestapo had failed to find out the true identities of the two men. Removing the poster was in itself a daring move and Violette ran a considerable risk in doing so.

In June 1944 Violette and her two senior resistance colleagues were picked up from a remote field by a Lysander aircraft of no. 138 Special Duties Squadron and flown back to Britain, where she spent a brief time with her parents and child before setting off on her second mission. It was explained to her before she set out that this mission was infinitely more dangerous than the first, and before leaving Britain she made her will and arrangements for the disposal of her possessions in case she failed to return. She told her parents that under no circumstances were they to make inquiries about her fate, even if they never heard of her again.

She returned to Paris, again in the role of courier, with the same two resistance workers who had been her earlier companions. This time, because of the danger of their being recognized, they were to go not to Rouen but to another resistance group in central France, in the area south of Châteauroux. The date was 7 June, and the Allies had gone ashore in Normandy twenty-four hours earlier. The principal task of Violette and her companions was to instruct the various resistance groups in planned attacks on German lines of communication and convoys moving up reinforcements to oppose the Allied landings in Normandy. They jumped from a Liberator bomber and received a tumultuous welcome from the Maquis, who had only just received news of the invasion.

The next few days were hectic ones; since the resistance groups were spread over a wide area the task of acquainting them with the directions from London was not easy. Violette employed a guide, a young Frenchman called Jacques Dufour, known by the code name of Anastasie. They set out on their round trip in an old car, and the first stage of their trip was accomplished without incident. Then, as they rounded a bend, they ran into a German patrol. They jumped out of the car and fled across a cornfield amid a hail of bullets. Violette was hit in the arm and then she sprained her ankle and collapsed among the corn, unable to go any further. Dufour wanted to carry her, but she persuaded him to make his escape while she held off the Germans for as long as possible.

For the next few minutes she carried on a one-sided battle, firing her Sten gun until her ammunition ran out. Dufour succeeded in getting away, but Violette was captured and taken by the Germans to the prison at Limoges, where she was handed over to the Gestapo. French resistance workers already had this prison under close surveillance and they reported that they had seen Violette being dragged across the courtyard on two successive days to the Gestapo offices. Their leaders immediately planned a rescue attempt for the third day, but this was forestalled when, at dawn, she was sent to

Paris under escort to undergo a more searching interrogation. She was thrown into Fresnes Prison, from where she was taken every day to the Gestapo headquarters in the Avenue Foch. There for several weeks she underwent the most brutal torture, but although the Gestapo succeeded in breaking her body they could never break her spirit and she revealed nothing of what she knew about the resistance movement.

Soon after her twenty-third birthday, hardly able to walk, she was put on a train for Germany together with two other female agents, Lilian Rolfe and Danielle Block. They were to be her constant companions throughout the ordeal that was to follow. There were also twenty-seven British officers on the train. Most of them had been involved in French resistance activities in one way or another and they were now destined for the men's section of the concentration camp at Buchenwald. Violette managed to contact them and found several old friends among them, including Wing Commander Yeo-Thomas, later to become famous as the 'White Rabbit', who was the senior British prisoner on the train. The journey was a nightmare, for it was now August 1944 and Allied fighter-bombers were constantly attacking all road and rail communications in northern France. The train stopped repeatedly while air attacks were in progress, but although the guards took shelter in the ditches alongside the railway track the prisoners remained locked in their fetid cars.

After several days of travelling under fearful conditions the train ended its journey at the women's death camp of Ravensbruck, north of Berlin, a great sprawling complex of huts dominated by a crematorium. At that time Ravensbruck housed over 25,000 women of all ages and nationalities. After several weeks in this man-made hell Violette and her two companions were sent to a labour camp at Torgau, where male and female concentration-camp inmates were set to work in a factory turning out precision instruments. This seemed to Violette to be the ideal opportunity to make an escape attempt and she set about evolving a plan, but she came under suspicion and soon afterwards she and the other two girls were sent back to the main camp at Ravensbruck. From there they were taken to another camp at Königsberg in northern Prussia, where they were employed, together with hundreds of other women, in felling trees to clear a site for use as an airfield. The weather was bitterly cold and the women – starved, beaten and brutally treated – died like flies, but although Lilian collapsed and became too weak to move, Danielle and Violette managed to hold out and fight their way through each fearful day.

By the middle of January 1945 the Russian Army was rapidly approaching Ravensbruck from the east, and for Violette and her two companions this in itself amounted to a death sentence. The camp commandant of Ravensbruck received direct orders from Berlin that the three girls were to be executed. They were taken back to the men's camp at Ravensbruck and placed in the death cells, where they were not allowed to be visited by any of the other prisoners. On 26 January 1945 they emerged from their cells – with Lilian supported between Violette and Danielle – and walked for the last time across the camp to the crematorium compound. The death sentence was read out to them and they were ordered to stand with their faces against a cement wall. There their young lives ended in a rattle of machine-gun fire, and afterwards their bodies were burned.

The courage of the three girls so impressed itself on the minds of their German guards that the latter gave full descriptions of their last movements under interrogation over a year later, and it was only then that the world knew the full story of the courage and subsequent fate of Violette Szabo. Today that courage is commemorated by a plaque in Lambeth town hall, near the place in which Violette spent her childhood. Every year, on the anniversary of her death, flowers are placed beneath the plaque in memory of a lovely young woman who should have had a whole world of happiness before her, but who instead found only death and horror at the hands of the most brutal regime in history.

NOOR INAYAT KHAN

The second of the posthumous George Crosses to be awarded to one of the courageous women of the French section of the Special Operations Executive went to Assistant Section Officer Noor Inayat Khan, Women's Auxiliary Air Force, known throughout her resistance career by the code name of Madeleine. Although her award was the last to be gazetted, on 5 April 1949, she was in fact the first woman radio operator to be infiltrated into enemy-occupied France, being landed by a Lysander of 138 Squadron on 16 June 1943. Her citation reads :

During the weeks immediately following her arrival the Gestapo made massive arrests in the Paris Resistance groups to which she had been detailed. She refused however to abandon what had become the principal and most danger-ous post in France, although given the opportunity to return to England, because she did not wish to leave her French comrades without communications and she hoped also to rebuild her group. She remained at her post there-fore and did the excellent work which earned her a post-humous Mention in Despatches.

The Gestapo had a full description of her but knew only her code name, Madeleine. They deployed considerable forces in their effort to catch her and so break the last remain-ing link with London. After three and a half months she was

betrayed to the Gestapo and taken to their headquarters in
the Avenue Foch. The Gestapo had found her codes and
messages and were now in a position to work back to
London. They asked her to co-operate but she refused and
gave them no information of any kind. She was imprisoned
in one of the cells on the 5th Floor of the Gestapo headquarters and remained there for several weeks, during which
time she made two unsuccessful attempts to escape. She
was asked to sign a declaration that she would make no
further attempts, but she refused, and the Chief of the
Gestapo obtained permission from Berlin to send her to
Germany for safe custody. She was the first agent to be
sent to Germany.

Assistant Section Officer Inayat Khan was sent to Karlsruhe in November 1943 and then to Pforzheim, where her
cell was apart from the main prison. She was considered to
be a particularly dangerous and un-co-operative prisoner.
She refused to give information either as to her work or her
colleagues. On 12 September 1944 she was taken with three
others to Dachau camp and on arrival there was taken to
the crematorium and shot. Assistant Section Officer Inayat
Khan displayed the most conspicuous courage, both
moral and physical, over a period of more than twelve
months.

Noor Inayat Khan came from a background that was different in every way from that of Violette Szabo. She was the
daughter of a wealthy Indian who later became a religious
mystic and travelled widely round the world. In the course
of these travels, in New York, he met and married Miss Ora
Baker, the niece of Mary Baker Eddy, founder of the Christian
Science Movement.

Noor was born on 1 January 1914 in the Kremlin in
Moscow, where her parents were the guests of Count Tolstoy.

She spent part of her childhood during World War One in Britain, but in 1920 her family went to live in France on the outskirts of Paris and it was here that she spent her adolescence. She was a beautiful, charming girl possessing a deep appreciation of things spiritual, which led her to love poetry and music. She attended the Academy of Music in Paris and in her early years composed several works of her own.

In fact it seemed that poetry and music were to form the pattern of her life, but the course of events was to change all that. In 1940 the Germans attacked on the western front, and on the collapse of France Noor's family were evacuated to Britain, where her brother joined the Royal Air Force and she enlisted in the WAAF. Because of her background and her ability to speak fluent French she, like Violette Szabo, soon found her way to the Special Operations Executive, and in the Summer of 1942 she volunteered for training as a secret agent specializing in radio work, which had been her trade in the WAAF.

Her chance to return to France came in the Spring of 1943, when there was an urgent need for an extra wireless operator in one of the leading resistance groups in the Paris area. Since she was the only fully qualified operator then available in SOE she was asked to undertake the mission. SOE officers went to great lengths to explain the dangers to her, but she brushed these aside and expressed a complete willingness to undergo whatever hardships might be necessary. Shortly afterwards she took off for France one night in one of 138 Squadron's faithful Lysanders. There, as her citation states, she carried out the highly dangerous role of wireless operator for the three and a half months, daily risking detection by the Germans. Almost the entire German intelligence network in the Paris area was devoted to tracking down this elusive girl, known only by the code name of Madeleine, but their investigations drew a blank until in October 1943 she was betrayed by a desperate Frenchwoman in return for a small amount of money, and arrested.

Even the Germans could not conceal their admiration for her exemplary conduct and courage after capture, and for the way she tried time and time again to escape. This admiration was also expressed by the governor of Pforzheim Prison, where she was kept in solitary confinement for nine months, much of it in chains. During this period of imprisonment she was a great source of strength to other French Resistance workers in the jail, contacting them by means of messages scratched on the back of her tin feeding bowl.

Her end was inevitable. In September 1944 she was taken to Dachau concentration camp together with three other resistance workers, Yolande Beekman, Eliane Plewman and Madeleine Dammerment. They arrived in the camp at midnight, and at dawn the next day they were taken out into the yard and forced to kneel down in the crematorium compound. They knelt two by two, holding hands in silence. They were each shot in the back of the neck.

In July 1967 a memorial ceremony was held at the house in Paris that had been Noor Inayat Khan's home before her family fled from France in 1940. A commemorative plaque was fixed to the boundary wall near the entrance and the ceremony was attended by the Indian ambassador, the attaché at the British Embassy and a number of other dignitaries including Colonel Buckmaster, who had been the head of the French section of SOE during the war. During the ceremony the latter read out the following message from Brigadier Sir John Smyth vc, the president of the Victoria Cross and George Cross Association:

> I and all the members of my Association, both holders of the Victoria Cross and the George Cross, will always revere Noor Inayat Khan GC and cherish her memory as one of

the most splendid and gallant women in our history. In her life – and particularly in her incredibly valiant work for the Resistance – she was always utterly staunch and true to the cause of freedom and to the comrades who were working with her, and she faced her death with the same courage she had always shown in her life.

Such was the calibre of the women who willingly gave their lives that others might live in freedom.

ODETTE

On 28 April 1912 a daughter was born to Gaston and Yvonne Brailly in the French town of Amiens. The child was baptized into the Catholic Church and given the names Odette Marie Céline. Two years later the child's father marched off to war and fought his way unscathed through the blood and carnage of Verdun, only to be killed at the very end of the battle by a shell while trying to save the lives of two wounded men from his platoon.

For little Odette the years of childhood were marked by periods of misery. When she was eight years old she went blind, and it was only the skill of a back-street herbalist, who offered to treat her when all the specialists had failed, that eventually restored her sight. A few months later the potions of this same man restored her to health and vigour when a bout of rheumatic fever left her weak and partly paralysed.

The happy times only really began when Odette was fourteen and the family moved to Boulogne. The girl, who attended a convent school, showed talent in a surprising number of directions. She loved music and horses and had a keen appreciation of the beauties of nature, delighting particularly in taking long, solitary walks along the picturesque coast. It would not be true to say that she was a popular girl, for she was moody, argumentative and headstrong, subject to sudden bouts of temper that made her unsuited to social conversation. It was perhaps unfortunate that her colleagues seldom saw the deeper, more understanding side of her nature, which she reserved for her times of solitude.

In 1930 Odette met Roy Sansom, an Englishman and the son of an old family friend. A year later they were married in the Church of Saint-Pierre and set up their home in Boulogne. Their first daughter, Françoise, was born in 1932 and shortly afterwards Odette crossed the Channel to make her home in Britain. A second daughter, Lily, was born in 1934 and she was joined by yet another girl, Marianne, in 1936. By this time the war clouds were gathering over Europe, and when the storm finally broke in September 1939 Odette made a similar contribution to the war to that of many other British housewives, donating blood to the local hospital, providing space in her house for children who were awaiting evacuation and handing over aluminium utensils to government collectors to be melted down and turned into Spitfires.

In April 1940 the period known as the phoney war came to a brutal end when the Germans struck in Norway, and a month later the Panzer divisions swept through Belgium and northern France. Within a month the British Expeditionary Force had retreated from Dunkirk and the German spearheads were sweeping southwards across the Somme, driving into the very heartland of Odette's country. Paris fell and on 22 June, with the signing of the Franco-German Armistice, Britain stood alone against the combined might of Germany and fascist Italy. In August 1940 the Luftwaffe began its blitz on Britain and in October, with a rain of high explosives falling nightly on London, Odette and her three daughters moved to a safer place in Somerset, not far from the home of her mother-in-law. It was a strangely idyllic existence, with half of Europe under the Nazi heel only a few short miles of water away and the culture of old Europe collapsing in blood and ruin.

In the Spring of 1941 Greece and Crete fell, and with his southern flank secured Hitler now turned on the Soviet Union, the victorious Wehrmacht rolling across the broad Russian steppes towards Moscow and Kiev. The Germans seemed to be winning on every front – and yet, in the occupied countries, their rear was being threatened by a rising tide of anger and hatred. In France the shock of the lightning campaign of 1940 and the subsequent invasion was beginning to wear off, and isolated incidents of resistance were starting to coalesce into a well-organized underground network. If one day the Allies were to re-establish a foothold on the Continent and drive back the invader, the activities of this resistance network had to be encouraged and nurtured until it became a powerful and effective striking force in the very heart of Nazi-dominated territory.

Such was the goal of the London-based SOE, the Special Operations Executive, whose French section was under the command of the famous Colonel Maurice Buckmaster, formerly intelligence officer to the 50th Northumbrian Division. In the Spring of 1941 SOE was in its infancy, the headquarters staff of the French section consisting of only four people, with ten hand-picked agents training somewhere in Britain in readiness to be parachuted into occupied France. Such were the beginnings of the secret army whose cloak was darkness, whose weapons were the bomb, pistol and dagger and whose password was courage.

In the Spring of 1942 Odette had not yet heard of SOE. She did, however, hear a radio broadcast by a naval commander who described a recent combined operations raid on Bruneval, where commandos and RAF experts had dismantled a secret German radar station and shipped it back to

Britain. He told how the raid had been meticulously planned with the aid of photographs, and appealed for anyone who might have prewar snapshots of the French coast or the areas behind it to send them to the Admiralty, where intelligence officers could conceivably use them in planning future operations. Odette had a number of such photographs and she decided to send them off. However she got the address wrong, and instead of going to the Admiralty they reached the War Office, together with Odette's covering letter in which she explained that she had lived in Boulogne for four years and knew that part of the coast intimately. Shortly afterwards a certain Major Guthrie wrote to Odette and invited her to call at his office for an interview. In the course of this and subsequent interviews she indicated her willingness to help the cause of France in any way possible. Finally she was introduced to Buckmaster, and so embarked on her career as an operative of the French section of the Special Operations Executive.

After some weeks she left for the SOE training school in the New Forest, having lost her identity and become known simply as Céline – or by the harsher designation of Agent 523 in the files of SOE. She was not an exemplary student. The report on her which was sent to Buckmaster at the end of her course read:

> Céline has enthusiasm and seems to have absorbed the teaching given on the course. She is however impulsive and hasty in her judgements and has not quite the clarity of mind which is desirable in subversive activity. She seems to have little experience of the outside world. She is excitable and temperamental, though she has a certain determination. A likeable character and gets on well with most people. Her main asset is her patriotism and her keenness to do something for France; her main weakness is her complete unwillingness to admit that she could ever be wrong.

That report very nearly spelled the end of Odette's career with SOE. There was no room in the organization for stubbornness, mistakes or over-hasty decisions. It was only her powers of persuasion and Colonel Buckmaster's shrewd judgement of character that saved the day. Until then she had no idea how close she had come to failure, and she left Buckmaster's office a very subdued woman.

From the New Forest school she went to the parachute training centre at Ringway, where she found her training something of an ordeal. Here, for the first but not the last time, fate was unkind to her : while making a practice jump from a mock-up of a Whitley bomber on the ground she smashed her face badly on the side of the exit hole and sprained her ankle on hitting the ground after a drop of about 8 feet. She spent some time in hospital recovering from this mishap and never went back to Ringway. Instead Buckmaster promised to find some other means of getting her into France. Apart from her parachute training, her identity of Céline was also left behind at Ringway. From now on she would be known as Lise.

In September 1942 she was given orders for her first operational mission. This involved flying to Gibraltar, from where she would then be taken by felucca, an Arab fishing boat, to a point on the French Mediterranean coast where she would be received by resistance workers who would enable her to contact the SOE operative who was to be her leader in France. His code name was Raoul, and his real name was Captain Peter Churchill. Raoul would give her details of how best to pass the demarcation line between Vichy and occupied France, and she was to set up her headquarters in Auxerre. Her cover story had been built up meticulously. She was to masquerade as a widow named Odette Metayer who had been born in Dunkirk in April 1912. As she read her cover story for the first time she realized that it was an extremely skilful blend of truth and fiction, following her own early career very closely.

On 17 September 1942 she arrived at Swindon airfield in Wiltshire and climbed aboard the Whitley that was to take her to Gibraltar. Even now fate seemed to be against her. As the Whitley taxied out for take-off it collided with another aircraft and slewed off the runway, one of its wings buckled. No other aircraft was available for the mission so Odette had no alternative but to return to London. A second attempt was fixed for the nineteenth. This time Odette was to fly by a Lysander of 138 Squadron to the Mâcon area, after which she was to make her way to Cannes and contact Raoul. She was about to board the aircraft when a warning came through from SOE headquarters at the very last minute. Apparently the Gestapo had swooped and rounded up the reception committee that was waiting to welcome Odette. Three of the group had already been killed and the others were in prison awaiting interrogation and eventually execution.

After yet another nerve-racking delay she went to an RAF airfield in Cornwall, where another Whitley bomber was waiting to carry out the original mission of flying her to Gibraltar. This time nothing could go wrong – or so she thought. The engines roared healthily and the aircraft thundered along the runway, gathering speed. It lifted into the air cleanly – then one of the engines cut out, and seconds later the aircraft struck the ground violently in a belly landing. The occupants scrambled from the wreck. It was pouring sheets of rain, and through it Odette saw to her horror that the aircraft had come to a dead stop on the very edge of a cliff with a sheer drop of 100 feet to the rocks and foaming sea below. Dimly, as she was led away from the wreck, she began to comprehend that fate was perhaps not so unkind to her after all.

She eventually arrived in Gibraltar in October and was picked up by the fishing boat on schedule. After four days at sea she was landed by dinghy on the French coast, together with another agent. The sailors who had brought them slipped away and they were left alone in the darkness, back once more in the country Odette loved. She was contacted by the resistance and made an uneventful journey to Cannes, where she met Raoul. From there she travelled to Marseilles, where she made further contacts and carried out work of a temporary nature while waiting to cross the border to Auxerre and begin her main mission. One of her tasks, together with Raoul, was to reconnoitre potential landing fields for the RAF's special duties aircraft. On one occasion, while waiting with a group of resistance workers for a Lysander to land, they were almost captured by Vichy French Milice who were working for the Gestapo and who had been tipped off that an aircraft was coming in. Odette and the others all managed to get away in the woods, but it was a close call.

In February 1943 the Gestapo launched an all-out attempt to net Raoul and his resistance group. Odette and the others had no alternative but to disband the network in the Cannes and Marseilles area and travel to Annecy, where they planned to begin their work all over again. They had learned from their previous mistakes, and this time they were determined that nothing should go wrong. The Cannes Resistance group had been too concentrated, and it was obvious that a wider dispersal of the resistance groups would be necessary if they were to elude the clutches of German Intelligence.

The first step was to select a series of suitable parachute-dropping zones, over forty of them in fact, which were to be listed and pinpointed for London. A different time schedule had to be worked out for each dropping zone so that the BBC could advise the resistance by coded message when a drop was to be made. A complex system was worked out whereby London was informed exactly what the reception committee at each dropping zone required in the way of material. Some

E

asked for Sten guns, others for explosives, medical supplies, clothes, radio sets, boots, commando knives and hand-grenades. For several weeks the Annecy area was the scene of intense resistance activity as couriers from the underground cells all over the country came and went. Plans were laid for the large-scale sabotage of railways. Everyone knew that the Allied invasion was coming but no one knew when, and the Resist-ance had to be prepared to play its part to the full. Once the network of dropping zones had been set up, London acted quickly. One night in March a formation of Halifaxes of the RAF's special duties squadrons dropped 126 containers to the Maquis groups in the hills round Annecy. Odette, lying in bed in the Hôtel de la Poste in Saint-Jorioz, heard the thunder of engines as the aircraft passed overhead and tears came into her eyes as she thought of the joy that the supplies would bring to the resistance workers.

During all this time German Intelligence continued its stren-uous efforts to break Raoul's resistance circuit. Leading the German drive was Hugo Bleicher, a senior officer in the Abwehr, the German Military Intelligence Service. Before long his agents had succeeded in infiltrating Raoul's group and he himself travelled to Annecy to make a first-hand appraisal of the situation. By the second week in April it was clear to Odette and her colleagues that it was time to move on again before the Germans swooped. They were too late. On the night of 16 April 1943 both Peter Churchill and Odette were arrested by Bleicher's agents and taken to the infamous Fresnes Prison near Paris.

Odette's initial interrogation was undertaken by Bleicher himself, and to her surprise the German officer showed her a considerable amount of courtesy. This she felt was because Bleicher was an Abwehr officer, and the Abwehr traditionally despised the Gestapo and their interrogation methods. Al-though at this stage she was not ill-treated the nights in

Fresnes Prison were a nightmare, with female SS warders tramping along the corridors and continually screaming commands at the other unfortunate inmates. Often the nights were punctuated by shrill screaming as the SS women vented their spite on some prisoner. Bleicher made determined attempts to persuade Odette to talk, stressing that if she failed to do so he would have no alternative but to hand her over to the Gestapo. Nevertheless she refused; the outcome was inevitable.

On the morning of 25 May 1943 she was taken before an SS tribunal at the Gestapo interrogation centre at no. 84 Avenue Foch. There, one by one, they pulled out her toenails with pincers. Despite the agony, which spread through her whole body, she made no sound. Afterwards she sat there in her wooden chair, her body quivering, looking down dumbly at the bloodstained floor. They gave her a cup of tea and she felt an irresistible urge to laugh, anything to give vent to the wave of sound that was striving to burst from her, but no murmur passed her lips – not even when they laid a red-hot poker across her spine. In the end they gave up and dragged her back to her cell, where she faced further persuasive interrogations from Bleicher – all in vain.

She remained in Fresnes Prison for a year and four days, resisting every attempt to make her reveal the secrets of her resistance organization. Finally, on 12 May 1944, she was put on a train together with other captured resistance workers under heavy SS guard. The SS left the prisoners in no doubt what their fate was to be. As the train moved east and they passed one station where the marshalling yards had been shattered by bombing, one of the SS guards turned to Odette and said : 'That is the work of the RAF. They have also destroyed my mother's house in Dortmund. I only wish an accident could happen to the train, for if it did, it would give me great pleasure to crush your skull under my heel and save the German hangman a job.'

After a fearful journey through the night, during which Odette suffered considerable pain from her handcuffs – which were clamped so hard on her wrists that the bones were bruised – the train reached Karlsruhe. There Odette was flung into the criminal prison, where she remained until mid-July, undergoing another series of interrogations. She never again saw any of the other prisoners who had accompanied her. Finally she was put on another train, which lurched its way along the bomb-torn railways of Germany and eventually arrived in the shattered ruins of Frankfurt. There Odette was locked in a prison cage like an animal, along with two women who were crawling with lice. She was forced to sleep on the stone floor and her daily diet consisted of three raw potatoes. At last, in the early hours of one morning, she was transferred to a place that had become synonymous with living hell for countless thousands of women from all over occupied Europe : Ravensbruck concentration camp. She arrived there in the evening of 18 July 1944, after a 3-mile march from the rail halt that set her badly mutilated feet aflame. There she was thrown into one of the dormitory blocks with a crowd of Ukrainian women, who kept up a continual mournful wailing. She was too tired to take any notice of them and fell into a deep and exhausted sleep.

There were more interrogations, all of which failed to produce any reaction from her. The result was that she was thrown into one of the deepest cells in the bunker, Ravensbruck's prison block. There she was forced to live for three and a half months in complete darkness, broken only by blinding flashes of light as a grill opened and one of the wardresses pushed in her scant rations. Through the fearful darkness there rang the screams of women who were being flogged and tortured. Unconsciously, time after time, she found herself counting the strokes as whiplashes bit into the lacerated flesh of some unfortunate's back and she found herself praying for the prisoner to lapse into unconsciousness so that the awful screaming would stop.

The landings of the British, French and American troops on the southern coast of France on 15 August 1944, was marked by a wave of brutality against the concentration-camp inmates. At Ravensbruck the central heating, controlled from outside Odette's cell, was turned up to full strength so that the room, which was normally icy, became an inferno. In desperation Odette soaked her blankets in cold water and wrapped herself in them, alternately burning and shivering. She was deliberately starved for a week, finally sinking into a kind of dazed coma. It almost killed her, though somehow she survived. In the wake of her starvation came a racking cough and scurvy spread over her whole body, while recurrent dysentery made every hour a nightmare. In September she was given perfunctory treatment in the camp hospital, then thrown back into her cell again. Every month she was visited by the camp commandant, Fritz Suhren. The interview was always brief and followed the same pattern. The commandant would stand in the door of her cell and ask : ' Is everything all right?' 'Yes, thank you.' 'Do you wish anything?' 'No, thank you.'

She hated his visits, for at least in the darkness and solitude of her cell she could escape within herself, dreaming of clear skies and spring time and of the day when the war would end. On the way back from the camp hospital to her cell she had found a leaf blowing across the dusty compound. She kept it by her in the darkness, fondled it, imagined it with a myriad other leaves and a forest of trees blowing in the wind, and this thought kept her sane.

Winter came, bringing with it penetrating cold. As the Allies advanced on Germany from all sides the brutality of the SS guards knew no bounds. In January 1945 Ravensbruck echoed to the daily rattle of gunfire as the German execution squads carried out their terrible work. Every day Odette expected to be dragged from her cell, put up against a wall and shot – yet somehow she continued to survive. A crisis came in April, when a direct order came from Heinrich Himmler that every living soul imprisoned in the bunker at Ravensbruck was to be killed. No witnesses were to be left to testify to the dreadful conditions of the concentration camp. The order was carried out to the letter, with seven exceptions; Odette was one of them. Why Fritz Suhren had spared her and six others she never learned.

At midnight on 27 April, the eve of her thirty-third birthday, Suhren came to her cell. He was alone. He stood in the door and gazed at her for some time, then he told her that she would be leaving the following morning at 6 o'clock. Together with several other inmates she was put into a closed truck that nosed its way out through the prison gates. Ravensbruck was in total confusion, for as the Allies approached the camp the SS were running away, stripping off their uniforms and escaping into the surrounding countryside, wearing whatever nondescript clothing they could find.

Odette was taken to another concentration camp at Neustadt, where she and the other occupants of the truck were locked in one of the huts. Like Ravensbruck this camp was in a turmoil, the SS guards having abandoned it and withdrawn beyond the perimeter where they waited in silence, their machine-guns trained on the compound while the inmates went wild. Early on 2 May a new convoy of male prisoners arrived at the camp, and as the gates were opened to admit them the other inmates rushed forward. At once the SS machine-guns opened fire, mowing down the prisoners in their dozens. From her window Odette saw the pathetic bundles in their striped prison rags strewn across the compound, their blood soaking into the dust.

On the afternoon of the following day an SS man kicked open the door of her hut and ordered her to accompany him.

He escorted her to the gate of the camp. There she saw three cars, the first and last full of uniformed SS troops. In the middle car sat Fritz Suhren, who ordered her to get in. For two hours they drove over the countryside, eventually arriving at a wood. There the little convoy stopped and Suhren ordered her to get out. She did so with trembling legs, certain that she was about to be shot. Miraculously, nothing of the sort happened. Instead Suhren took a pile of papers from his briefcase, stacked them beside a tree and set fire to them. Then, even more amazingly, he produced a bottle of wine and a pack of sandwiches, which he shared with Odette. Then the convoy was on the move again, driving at high speed along the deserted road.

Odette slumped in her seat, overwhelmed by utter exhaustion, too tired to care about her fate. They drove on until at dusk they came to within sight of a village, where the cars slowed down and finally stopped. Rousing herself from her stupor, Odette looked ahead. The road through the village was straddled by a group of soldiers wearing drab, unfamiliar uniforms. They carried Tommy guns. Suhren got out of the car and motioned for Odette to do the same. Approaching the strange men, the former commandant of Ravensbruck said: 'This is Frau Churchill. She has been a prisoner. She is a relation of Winston Churchill, the Prime Minister of England.' Astonished, the Americans regarded this battered scarecrow of a woman. After a few seconds the scarecrow spoke: 'And this is Fritz Suhren, commandant of Ravensbruck concentration camp. Please make him your prisoner.' Then, desperately tired, she turned and walked back to the car.

So ended the months of bravery and torment that, after the war, were to earn Odette Sansom the award of the George Cross. As she sat in Suhren's car on that fateful May evening, watching darkness creep over the land while the Americans checked out her story, one of the SS men who had accompanied her came over and spread a sheepskin flying-jacket over her knees to keep her warm. It seemed a genuine gesture, and she fell asleep marvelling at the strangeness of human nature. Perhaps, after all, there was hope for the world of tomorrow.

9 Resistance Nurse

Nurses, generally, are a courageous breed. Nowhere does this truth emerge more strongly than in the story of Alexandrina Marsden – an elderly Englishwoman whose traditional hatred of oppression and brutality, together with a deep dedication to her profession, brought her to do battle in her own way against the enemy.

E*

In May 1940, while Nancy Wake was driving her ambulance along the bullet-raked roads of Belgium, an Englishwoman named Alexandrina Marsden was also doing her bit for the Allied cause as a nurse in the hospital at Dinard. The two women were destined never to meet, and in many respects they were poles apart. For a start, Alexandrina – at the age of sixty-three – was old enough to be Nancy's grandmother. Moreover she came from a totally different background, having been brought up in the India of the British Raj at the turn of the century. Her father was a regular army officer with the Bengal Lancers on the staff of Lord Roberts. In other ways, however, she and Nancy were completely as one. Both were courageous and both were completely dedicated to the task in hand, imbued with a fierce determination to see it through to the end, no matter what dangers and obstacles might lie in their path.

Both, too, possessed a consuming hatred for the Germans. As a child, Alexandrina had been sent to a boarding-school in Germany and the harsh treatment meted out by the staff to the pupils had left a lasting mark on her. In the end her pride had caused her to rebel against the system, and when the German crown prince arrived to inspect the school one day she flatly refused to curtsey to him as she had been ordered, a move that resulted in her immediate expulsion. On leaving school she developed a deep admiration for nursing and became increasingly determined to follow in the footsteps of Florence Nightingale and Elizabeth Garrett Anderson. Her mother was totally opposed to the idea, maintaining that nurs-

ing was no profession for a girl of Alexandrina's breeding and
education. Although she was infuriated by this snobbish
attitude, which was quite prevalent among the English upper
classes at the time, Alexandrina temporarily gave in and
at the turn of the century travelled to India for an extended
stay with relatives. There she met Captain Richard Marsden of the Royal Artillery, whom she married in November
1903.

In the idyll that followed she almost forgot about her
passion for nursing, but the turn of world events was soon to
bring it to the forefront of her mind once more. In August
1914 World War One broke out and Dick Marsden was
ordered to join the British Expeditionary Force in France.
Alexandrina at once decided to travel to Britain and renew
her attempts to become a nurse. According to *The Times*,
thousands of women were required to train as nurses with the
VAD – Voluntary Aid Detachment – for service at home and
in France, and it was with high hopes that Alexandrina went
to the Middlesex Hospital and volunteered her services to the
matron.

Although she was taken on she soon found that the presence
of VADs under training was greatly resented by professional
nurses, many of whom went out of their way to be aggressive
and unpleasant. She was given the dirtiest and most unpleasant
jobs to do but she managed to bear her treatment stoically,
until she was obliged to go on sick-leave with a septic throat.
On her return she was transferred to the out-patients depart-
ment, where the treatment she received from other members
of the staff was a distinct improvement. Here, for the first time,
she was allowed to handle the patients, performing simple
tasks like changing dressings, syringeing ears and administering
medicines. Many of the patients were from the London slums
and their condition was horrifying, but Alexandrina soon
became accustomed to the fearful sights she encountered and

her training was to stand her in invaluable stead when, in 1915, she received orders to move to France.

She was to spend nearly three years of almost unbroken service on the western front in hospitals and dressing stations close to the front line, patching together the flotsam of total war. For weeks on end, when the Allies or the Germans were in the middle of an offensive, she worked almost without sleep along with other British VADs and French nurses. Every day men were brought in from the trenches in huge convoys, and she soon found that there were more victims of disease, gas and frostbite than of shell and bullet. In the nightshift operating theatre she witnessed sights that seemed to have come out of hell : amputations performed without anaesthetic, men blinded and maimed and screaming in their abject terror. Later she wrote :

> I shall never forget the endless stream of wounded pouring into our hospital during the five months of the Battle of the Somme. They arrived literally by the hundred and, as at Florence Nightingale's hospital at Scutari, were bedded down in every available corner of the hospital. As we were still suffering from a shortage of both nurses and supplies we were desperately inadequate for such a situation. Very often we were obliged to work 24 hours at a stretch without even a break for proper meals. We rushed from patient to patient dressing wounds, administering sedatives and generally doing the best we could to make them comfortable. We worked at tremendous pressure but in the midst of such tragedy our own tiredness seemed of little importance.

Such was the daily pattern of Alexandrina's life until early in 1918, when once more she developed a septic throat and had to be invalided home. In nearly three years of nursing she had had only a fortnight's leave.

On her recovery she took up an appointment as sister in

charge at an auxiliary military hospital in Cheshire. Then came the Armistice in November 1918, and soon afterwards the well-deserved award of the Croix de Guerre with Palms. Her husband Dick, now a colonel, was in Ireland as command-ing officer of the Curragh military camp. Some time later Dick resigned from the army and the couple set up home in the beautiful county of Kildare. Even then they were not free from danger, for Ireland was torn by civil war and strife as Irish terrorists fought the British security forces and one another. Nevertheless Dick and Alexandrina survived it all and re-mained in Ireland until 1938, when they went to live in Brittany.

Alexandrina had left France towards the end of World War One only to return in time for the outbreak of World War Two. Despite her age, she at once volunteered for nursing duties in Dinard and was alarmed to find that conditions had not improved since the 1914-18 war. The French medical authorities gave her the task of converting a large hotel in the town with seven hundred beds into a hospital and appointed her matron. During the period of the 'phoney war' most of the casualties she and her staff had to deal with were French and British troops from the Maginot Line, with a few shot-down German airmen. Then, in May 1940, the Germans invaded France and the Low Countries and the spate of casualties began to mount. After that the collapse of the French armies was rapid, and although few of her French colleagues appeared to realize the full extent of the disaster it came as no surprise to Alexandrina when, on 22 June, the French government under Marshal Pétain signed an armistice with the Germans.

Shortly afterwards the hospital in Dinard was occupied by the Germans, who tried to persuade Alexandrina to work officially for them in her capacity as matron. She refused and was made prisoner, together with her husband. The two were taken to Dinant, but to their surprise they found that far from being confined in some prison camp they were actually under open arrest, which meant that they could wander through the town and talk to the inhabitants at will. Alexandrina soon discovered that close to the town there was a large German camp hospital containing many British and French prisoners, and she determined to gain admission to the camp to see how the men were faring.

Wearing the uniform of a French nurse and with an arm-band with a black swastika that she had managed to obtain displayed on her arm, she walked through the gates of the camp and set about helping in any way she could. After her first visit she scouted round for suitable contacts from whom she might obtain food and other necessities for the prisoners. A priest introduced her to a local farmer, who volunteered to supply fruit, vegetables and, whenever he could spare them, eggs and meat. She also managed to secure chocolate and biscuits and the occasional packet of cigarettes, as well as other small luxuries. A local chemist promised to supply medicines, sedatives and bandages free of charge whenever she needed them. Armed with these odds and ends she visited the camp every day to give what comfort she could to the prisoners and change their dressings. The Germans never once challenged her. Officers either ignored her or nodded stiffly as she passed by while the nurses took her visits for granted, assuming her to be someone in authority.

It was her very self-confidence that proved to be her undoing. One day, when smuggling a letter from a Frenchwoman into the camp to give to the woman's two sons, she was challenged by a German guard and refused to stop. The guard at once arrested her and she was taken before the camp commandant. After hours of interrogation the Germans let her go, but from now on she was under constant surveillance and in November 1940 she and Dick were rounded up together with

thirty other British civilians and taken to the prison camp.
To her surprise the camp commandant, instead of having her
thrown into the cells, ordered her to take charge of the British
prisoners. For a fortnight she did her best, caring for the sick
under conditions of extreme cold and inadequate feeding and
doing much to raise the prisoners' flagging morale. Then, on
4 December, she was informed that she and fifty British prisoners were to be transferred to another prison the next day.

The following morning, she mustered the fifty prisoners on
the frozen parade ground for final inspection. There they were
joined by a further hundred or so prisoners of various other
nationalities – French, Dutch, Belgian and Polish – who she
discovered were to accompany them on the journey to their
unknown destination. Once more, to her astonishment, the
camp commandant put her in charge of the whole party,
which was then driven to Dinant railway station and penned
in a wire enclosure together with another five hundred prisoners. Packed like sardines they stayed there for more than two
hours, shivering in the ice and snow, waiting for their train.
Only when they were on board did they learn that their destination was to be Frankfurt. Fear rippled through the crowd
of prisoners. To most of them their destination in Germany
meant only one thing – a concentration camp.

The train journey was a nightmare. There was no room to
sit down and the passengers, crammed into the small compart-
ments, suffered badly from extremes of heat and cold and also
hunger, for the Germans had not thought to provide any food.
During the day the train's heaters were turned up to suffoca-
tion point; then at night they were switched off. Several of
the passengers succumbed to this barbaric treatment and
Alexandrina did what she could to help them, but the German
doctor on the train refused to render any assistance and several
people died, including a young mother and her new-born
baby. At one halt Alexandrina managed to secure a few loaves

of French bread from some railway workers, who pushed them through the windows of her coach at the risk of their lives. It was the only food they had during the entire journey.

After three days and nights of agony the train pulled into the old French town of Besançon at the foot of the western Jura Mountains. There, to their relief, the passengers learned that there had been a change of plan. Instead of continuing to Frankfurt they were now to be interned in France. Conditions in the prison at Besançon, which had once been a laundry, were frightful and far worse than anything that had been experienced at Dinant. The Germans had turned two or three rooms into large dormitories and instead of bunks had strewn straw over the floor, on which the prisoners were expected to bed down.

On several occasions Alexandrina and the others were awakened by the sound of shrill screams echoing down the corridors of the old building. She had no idea how many prisoners were tortured or what form their tortures took, because the Germans took care to keep their victims apart from the other prisoners. Nevertheless, hearing those screams tearing through the building was a harrowing experience and she was conscious that she too might well have been one of those victims. Throughout this period she continued to make vehement protests to the camp commandant about conditions, and after two or three weeks the German officer, determined to be rid of this troublesome woman, despatched her to the local hospital to help with the nursing.

What Alexandrina had been called upon to endure at the hands of aggressive nurses during her early days in the 1914-18 war was as nothing compared with the brutal treatment she – and indeed the patients – received from the German nurses employed in the Besançon hospital. 'The German doctors,' she later wrote, 'were negligent in their duty and the German nurses downright brutal.' Alexandrina and some French nuns who had also volunteered were treated little better than slave labourers. They were kept on duty for cruelly long hours, with almost no sleep and very little food. Their staple food consisted of mangolds, mushy potatoes, bread and watery soup, a diet that soon reduced Alexandrina to a shadow of her former self. In the end she collapsed altogether and found herself among the patients whom she had been trying so valiantly to help. Fortunately the French nuns took her under their wing and during the three months when she hovered between life and death they looked after her day and night. Without them she could not possibly have survived.

Soon after her recovery in May 1941 she and Dick were reunited and transferred to Rennes in Brittany, where they were once again placed under open arrest. They were dumped unceremoniously in the middle of town with no food, no money, nowhere to live and orders to report to the local commandant every twenty-four hours. Fortunately after roaming the streets for several hours, they managed to find accommodation at a small inn used mainly by commercial travellers and run by Monsieur and Madame Alizon, a charming couple with two teenage daughters, Mariette and Simone. It was only after they had been there some time that Alexandrina and Dick realized what danger the Alizons were facing by sheltering the two British people. Both the Alizons were members of the French Resistance, and the very fact of sheltering two strangers under their roof meant that they were running incredible risks.

As soon as they found out the nature of the Alizons' activities, Alexandrina and Dick determined to move as quickly as possible. Soon afterwards there came a real windfall in the shape of a letter from a priest whom Alexandrina had known at Dinard and who now owned a house in Rennes. How he found out the whereabouts of the two British people remained a mystery; nevertheless what mattered was his offer of the loan of his property for as long as the two of them wanted it.

The Marsdens' friendship with the Alizons continued after they had moved into the priest's villa, and through them they gradually acquired a widening circle of friends, most of whom were connected with the Resistance in some capacity. As the months went by Alexandrina noticed that Madame Alizon was looking more frail and anxious, and when she visited her one morning she found her in a state of almost complete collapse. The distraught Frenchwoman told Alexandrina that the Gestapo had taken her two teenage children. The thought flashed through Alexandrina's mind that the Alizons were now probably paying the price for having befriended the British couple, but it later transpired that the Gestapo had been following the activities of Simone and Mariette for some time and had arrested them as soon as enough evidence had been assembled. Nevertheless Alexandrina determined to do all in her power to find out what had happened to the children. Running a considerable risk she went to see the local police, who told her that the children had been sent to Fresnes, one of the biggest and worst prisons in France, which was now full of Gestapo victims. Her pleas that Madame Alizon be allowed to see her children were to no avail and a couple of weeks later the Frenchwoman, broken in body and spirit, died.

Tragic though it was at the time, her death spared her the further horror of seeing her husband taken prisoner and her daughters transferred to the concentration camp at Auschwitz, where they suffered cruelly, one of them, Mariette, dying of her ill-treatment. Such incidents filled Alexandrina with horror and as time went by she became more and more involved with resistance activities, setting up a private clinic for victims of Gestapo torture. Many of them were in a pitiful state, and it was only the Englishwoman's prompt attention that saved them from permanent disfigurement.

Her involvement with the Resistance became deeper in the

Spring of 1942 when one morning she received a clandestine
visitor in the shape of a resistance operative working under
the code name of 'Saint-Jean'. He told her that the Rennes
section of the Resistance was setting up an escape line for shot-
down Allied airmen and escaping prisoners-of-war, and they
urgently needed someone who was familiar with the different
British dialects to interview airmen and other escapees who
purported to be British, and advise on whether they were
genuine or not. Alexandrina, with her distinctive nurse's uniform – which had proved to be as good as a passport to many
areas where ordinary civilians were denied access – seemed to
be the ideal person for the job. 'Saint-Jean' stressed that such
work would be dangerous that she should be prepared to be
called out at any time of the day or night, and that if she
should be caught she must deny that she was a member of the
Resistance. Nobody, he emphasized, would stand by her. She
might be tortured – perhaps sent to a concentration camp –
but she would receive no help from the Resistance if that happened, and nobody would admit her existence.

Despite this forbidding warning she readily agreed to help.
'Saint-Jean' was delighted and told her that the leader of the
Rennes section of the Resistance, a Madame Prudomme,
would call upon her later to discuss details of her work. She
had a simple French sentence to memorize. Whenever she
assisted in the escape of a British subject she had to make him
learn the phrase: *'Nous avons la confiance d'Anne de
Bretagne'*. If the escaper succeeded in reaching Britain the
BBC would broadcast these words over their European network as a signal of his safe return.

Less than twenty-four hours later, the grim truth of 'Saint-
Jean's' warning struck home when the Gestapo broke into
Madame Prudomme's flat and arrested her together with a
British soldier whom she had been hiding. The Englishman
was shot out of hand, Madame Prudomme was arrested and

sent to a concentration camp. Nothing more was ever heard of her. The Gestapo made a thorough search of her flat and confiscated everything they could find: funds, a code used for messages and other incriminating documents. During the next few days they rounded up nearly four hundred of the six hundred men and women of the Rennes Resistance, most of whom were shot without trial. Alexandrina was lucky. Madame Prudomme had had no time to commit the English-woman's name to paper. Such, in the wartime French Resistance, was the narrow dividing line between life and death.

The disruption of the resistance group by the Gestapo meant that for the time being Alexandrina and her colleagues dared not embark on any escape plans until the hue and cry had begun to die down. For four months they lay low, contenting themselves with ferreting out information about the Nazi defences in Rennes, the whereabouts of arms and supply dumps and other information that would be of use to the Intelligence staff in London. Miraculously, Alexandrina managed to keep her membership of the Resistance a secret from her husband throughout the entire war. If he had known the risks she was running he would almost certainly have done his best to stop her. When the four-month delay period was over and the escape network began to function again she would carry out her work of interrogating shot-down airmen at night, slipping out of the house while her husband snored in the next room, making her way to some secret rendezvous dressed in her nurse's uniform and armed with a small case of medical equipment as camouflage in case she was stopped by a German patrol.

Once an airman had been thoroughly vetted he was handed over to the care of a Frenchwoman named Madame Julien, and that was usually the last Alexandrina heard of him until the code message came over the BBC, revealing that he was safely back in Britain. In addition to her work in helping air-

men and prisoners to escape, a task that became little short
of momentous as Allied air raids over France intensified,
Alexandrina kept her eyes and ears open on her travels and
transmitted back to London an impressive list of German
installations, many of which were subsequently attacked and
destroyed by the Allied air forces. These messages were always
transmitted by another member of the resistance group, but
as Alexandrina became more proficient in coding techniques
and radio operation she was given a miniature transmitter to
take back to her house so that she could send future messages
to London herself. As it happened, she was never to have the
chance to use it. One morning the Gestapo appeared on her
doorstep and searched the house from top to bottom. Fortunately Alexandrina had had an opportunity to destroy the
transmitter and the Gestapo men left empty handed. But they
posted two sentries in her house to watch her movements day
and night; they stayed for four weeks before they were finally
withdrawn.

It was not long before the Gestapo caught up with her
again. One night, when making her way home through the
streets of Rennes after listening to the evening BBC broadcast at the house of a colleague, she was stopped by a German
patrol and arrested. She was taken to the office of the local
German commandant, who interrogated her for two hours,
but he could find no evidence against her and at last he was
compelled to let her go. Shortly afterwards she was once again
arrested, this time by the French Milice. She soon found that
these turncoat Frenchmen were far more dangerous even
than the Gestapo, for after she had been at their headquarters
for a short time an official announced without ceremony that
she was to be shot. She was dragged outside by three thugs
armed with Tommy guns and stood up against a wall. The
men backed off and raised their weapons. It never occurred to
Alexandrina to be frightened; all she felt was a deep astonish-

ment. Quietly she said 'Remember Nurse Cavell', referring to the British heroine who had been executed by the Germans during World War One. The men wavered, conferred among themselves and finally took her back indoors. After three more hours of confinement the Milice finally let her go.

In 1944, during the months leading up to D-Day, the British and United States Air Forces operated at maximum effort in an attempt to destroy as much of the German communications network in France as possible, and Alexandrina's resistance group was kept busy sending a steady flow of information on potential targets to London. It was now that the full horror of war came home to Alexandrina, for on several occasions sticks of bombs fell among the houses of Rennes itself, causing a great deal of devastation and many casualties. She herself often risked death to help the injured and dying while bombs still exploded all round. She was injured more than once, the first time by two small bomb splinters that struck her in the thigh. On another occasion her house received a direct hit, the bomb exploding in a room where she and her husband had been standing only a few moments before. As firemen rescued them from the debris Alexandrina noticed that blood was running down her face. A moment later she began to feel giddy and almost fainted. She was rushed to a makeshift hospital in a nearby convent, where it was found that she had wounds in the head and hip. An emergency trepanning operation saved her life, and during the lengthy period of recuperation in hospital she had plenty of time to reflect wryly that the Allies had inadvertently come far closer to killing her accidentally than the Germans had intentionally.

On her return home she immediately plunged into her underground work once more, finding her talents as a nurse more and more in demand as armed resistance groups in the area became more active and the Germans made a furious last-ditch attempt to wipe them out. There were frequent shooting incidents and it was by no means an uncommon occurrence for wounded Frenchmen to turn up on Alexandrina's doorstep begging for help. The air raids continued too, but one day the inhabitants of Rennes – who had grown used to the sound of crashing bombs – heard a different kind of explosion in the distance. It was the sound of American artillery, shelling the German defences in front of the town. Soon afterwards the Germans were in full retreat, and on the morning of 4 August a French Red Cross ambulance driver called at Alexandrina's house with a request that since she was British she should drive with him to Saissonne to make contact with the Americans. After an uneventful journey over a countryside that was tasting freedom for the first time in four years, she rode into Saissonne like a conquering heroine through lines of cheering people who threw flowers in her path.

Her war work was not yet over. After the Liberation Alexandrina assisted the Allies by compiling lists of known collaborators, and in furnishing evidence of Gestapo brutality which was later used at the Nuremberg war crimes trials. In recognition of her services the French awarded her the Croix de la Résistance and the British the MBE.

10 Survival in the Jungle

NONA BAKER KNEW NOTHING of the fearful tortures and executions that were the lot of the women who worked for the Resistance, nor did she come under fire. Hers was an ordeal of a different kind, an ordeal of privation and misery lasting four long years in the Malayan jungle, of helplessly watching her brother die by her side.

This story tells of a different kind of courage; the courage to endure, to survive each day with the sure knowledge that each successive day will be no better, and perhaps a lot worse, than the one before.

In the Autumn of 1941 the war on every front – in Russia, the Atlantic, North Africa and the Mediterranean – seemed to be going badly for the Allies.

Yet to Vincent Baker and his sister Nona, living a life of ease and luxury among the high society of British-ruled Malaya, the war news from Britain – though increasingly alarming – seemed as remote as the moon. Vincent Baker owned one of the largest tin mines in the country, and his sister, who was seventeen years his junior, enjoyed a style of living that – thanks to their not inconsiderable wealth – reflected the waning splendour of the British Raj. In fact the Sultan of Pahang, the state in which the tin mine was situated, was a frequent visitor to the Bakers' house, which was large and well equipped enough to cope with his forty-strong retinue.

All in all it seemed impossible that any major disturbance could threaten their prosperity and security, even though the expansionist aims of Japan in South-East Asia were causing Vincent and others like him a certain amount of worry. The Japanese threat had become more pronounced since June 1940, when, on the collapse of France, Indo-China had been handed over to the Japanese, which meant that only defence-less Siam stood between their armies and a possible invasion of Malayan territory. Nevertheless both Nona and her brother believed that such an invasion would be doomed to failure; troops had been pouring into Malaya from Britain, India and Australia, every town in the country was garrisoned, and – after all – everyone knew that one British soldier was worth at least four Japs. No one in Malaya, including the Bakers, had any idea how ill equipped their own troops were, or how proficient the Japanese had become.

Even when, on the morning of 8 December 1941, the news came through that the Japanese had attacked Pearl Harbour, that airfields on Singapore and the mainland had been bombed and that enemy forces had set foot in Malaya at Singora and Khota Bharu, they still did not realize the full extent of the disaster. It was only forty-eight hours later, with the devastating news that the battleships *Prince of Wales* and *Repulse* – on which British naval hopes in the Far East had been pinned – had been sunk by Japanese torpedo-bombers, that Vincent and Nona knew that it was only a matter of time before the Japanese advanced into the heart of Malaya. On the first signs of approaching danger they made plans to hide in the jungle for a while; even now, optimistically, they believed that it would be only a few weeks at the most before British forces advanced northwards from Singapore and drove the enemy out again.

During the last week of December Vincent received a telegram from the British Resident in Kuala Lipis ordering him to flood the tin mine. Soon afterwards he and Nona packed a few possessions and went into the jungle with Cheng Kam, their mine foreman, who had found a hut where they could lie low. It was a makeshift affair, consisting of little more than a roof of palm leaves with a frame braced against a tree and built on a flat rock overhanging a waterfall that tumbled into a deep gorge. The flimsy structure proved to be no protection against the downpour that came that first night, and the next few days were spent in misery as the heavy tropical rain soaked everything. Nona and Vincent both suffered from severe colds, but because of the risk of discovery there could be no question of lighting a fire and for weeks they shivered in their sodden clothing, growing steadily weaker despite the fact that Cheng Kam and one or two of his friends brought them food whenever possible.

Their despair reached new depths in the middle of February, when they learned that Singapore had fallen. For the first time they began to consider seriously whether it would be best to give themselves up to the Japanese. It was Cheng Kam who talked them out of the idea, explaining that several of their European friends had already been executed and that because of the authority Vincent had wielded they could expect a similar fate.

To cut down the risk of discovery by Japanese patrols Cheng Kam kept them moving from one hut to another. They began to lose all count of time; their only contact with the outside world was Cheng Kam, and as time went by – because of the danger that he might be arrested by the Japanese secret police – his visits became fewer. To compensate for the lack of food Vincent and Nona supplemented their diet with wild mangoes, but too many of these brought on severe attacks of dysentery, which added to their overall weakness.

As the weeks went by Nona became an increasing tower of strength as she anxiously noted a progressive deterioration in her brother's health. She had her own agony to bear, too; one day she upset the primus and over-turned a pan of boiling water on her leg, burning it so severely that she was unable to walk for several weeks. She had only just begun to recover when Vincent came down with a bad attack of malaria, raving in delirium and shivering so badly that he shook the entire hut. For days on end Nona lay beside him, holding him in her arms in an effort to keep him warm. Apart from a few M & B tablets they had no medicine, and it was not until the faithful Cheng Kam appeared one day with a small supply of quinine that the situation began to improve, although Vincent's attacks of malaria went on recurring at intervals.

For Nona the greatest torment was the rats – big jungle

creatures that made inroads into the food store and bit through mosquito nets. After the rats came the north-east monsoon, which turned everything to sodden pulp once more, and it was with considerable relief that they decided to risk lighting a fire in the evenings. The tiny, flickering flame brought with it a sense of comfort; for the first time since they left their home Nona began to feel strangely happy. The boredom that had been their constant companion was magically dispelled as she experimented with the small supply of food at her disposal, trying to make nourishing meals out of virtually nothing.

So the months passed, undisturbed by anything other than frequent discomfort. The year 1943 dawned – and suddenly, in February of that year, a crisis developed. A Malayan messenger arrived with the news that one of the workmen on Vincent's estate, who had got heavily into debt, had gone to Cheng Kam and told him that he would reveal the whereabouts of the British couple to the Japanese if the foreman did not pay him a considerable sum of money. Vincent and Nona realized that it was time to move on, and Vincent arrived at a momentous decision.

In the hills there were several groups of Chinese communists, who were fighting a guerrilla war against the Japanese, and in the interests of safety Vincent decided to join them. Nona knew full well what the decision must have cost him, for her brother had been anti-communist throughout his life and had always regarded the Malayan communists as despised agitators bent on overthrowing the established way of life.

The following day, with Chinese guides, Vincent and Nona set off through the jungle on the trek to the nearest communist camp. After several hours on the march they were suddenly confronted by an armed sentry, who emerged from the trees to bar their path; their guide shouted the password and they were led into a small clearing, occupied by a number of huts.

There were forty or so Chinese Malays working in the clearing, and the British couple were delighted to find that some of them had been employees at the mine. They received a tumultuous reception, and it was only when the noise had died down somewhat that they learned the shattering news that the Japanese now ruled the whole of south-east Asia from China down to New Guinea and across to the Indian border.

Vincent and Nona found themselves part of the regimented life of the communist camp under its leader, Lao Liu. There was no longer any privacy; at night they were accommodated in a hut with twenty Chinese, and in the mornings they were expected to take part in communal bathing. Nona was the only woman in the camp and no special arrangements were made for her, but since no one took the slightest notice of her she felt no embarrassment.

A day or two after their arrival the whole contingent moved to another camp, about four hours' march away, which was located in a safer position. The trek was hard, the trail winding round the crest of the hills that surrounded the Sungei Lembing Valley, which entailed either stiff climbing or dangerous descents and the crossing of a broad stream that had no bridge other than a tree trunk, slippery with moss and lichen. Time after time the two Europeans slipped and fell on the rocky, sodden ground until their hands and knees were raw and bleeding and they were covered in mud from head to foot.

Their stay in the new camp was destined to be short. After a couple of weeks they were ordered to move to the communist headquarters at Sungei Riau, which was deep in the jungle and considered to be a safer hiding-place. They set out with a party of twenty, all armed to the teeth. On the first day they crossed thickly wooded hills where the trail was almost hidden by great clumps of fern, sodden with rainwater, and clusters of a particularly nasty type of palm whose feathery fronds concealed hook-like thorns that buried themselves in the flesh. On the second day the going was even worse, with thunderstorms turning the dried-up river-bed they had been following into a flowing quagmire. By this time Vincent and Nona were exhausted, but the coming of night brought no respite, for it was essential to cross the River Kuantan before dawn using a temporary bridge built by the Japanese.

As they approached the river they went forward cautiously in single file, their eyes straining to penetrate the darkness, expecting to be ambushed by a Japanese patrol at any moment. Fortunately their luck held, and by sunrise they were safely in the jungle on the other side of the water. A few hours later they arrived at the new camp, to be greeted by the usual noisy reception. Vincent and Nona hardly noticed it; blind with exhaustion, they collapsed on the hard ground and let oblivion wash over them.

The Sungei Riau headquarters, from where the administration of all communist camps in Malaya's Pahang Province was carried out, was surprisingly well equipped. There was a parade ground, a radio shack, an administration block containing typewriters and duplicators requisitioned from the empty offices of the rubber plantations attached to Vincent's mine. From here propaganda leaflets were distributed all over the province by messengers sympathetic to the communist cause, who – in addition to this work – also acted as couriers on a jungle escape line for Malays who were threatened by the Japanese, as well as providing intelligence on Japanese troop movements and impending anti-guerrilla operations.

Nona and Vincent were well treated, being provided with fresh clothing and extra food whenever possible. Their condition soon improved and they plunged wholeheartedly into the life of the camp. One day, in the camp office, Nona found a sheet of paper with some music on it and unconsciously began to hum the tune; a moment later an excited camp commissar burst in and earnestly begged her to teach the song to the rest of his men. It was, in fact, the communist 'Internationale', which no one in the camp had so far been able to sing properly. Under Nona's tuition Sungei Riau's rendering of the Red hymn was soon the envy of all other camps in the area. She taught the guerrillas other songs, too – many with highly uncomplimentary words about the Japanese, set to well-known tunes.

By May 1943 there was an acute shortage of arms throughout the camp in Pahang Province, and the communist commander, hearing that a cache of weapons was concealed near Vincent's former home at Sungei Lembing, decided to go in search of it. Taking a large body of his best troops, together with Vincent and Nona, he set off into the jungle.

Nona found the going almost unbearably tough; a lot of trees had been felled across the trail, and since their trunks were covered in slime and moss negotiating them was an exhausting businesss. Apart from that, there were the leeches; Nona was so intent on keeping up with the party that it was hours before she saw, with horror, that the exposed parts of her body were festooned with the bloated creatures. By nightfall, when they arrived at a friendly small-holding, her arms and legs were covered in blood. Fortunately the farmer's wife knew the correct treatment : lighting a fire, she made a charcoal poultice and rubbed it on Nona's sores. Within a few hours the pain and inflammation had begun to die away.

The first expedition failed to find the weapons, but it had no sooner returned to camp than the commander, Lao Lee, determined to set out once more. The first trek had taken its toll of Vincent's strength and now he was too ill to leave the camp. The most miserable experience of Nona's life was to see him standing there, waving feebly as the others moved out later that day.

F

It took the second expedition twenty-four hours to cover the 30 miles between Sungei Riau and the patch of forest overlooking Sungei Lembing – quite a remarkable achievement in that rough terrain. After a short rest they began the search for the weapons, and hopes rose when a Chinese said that he had actually seen them being buried. After digging for some hours, however, they found nothing more exciting than a broken thermos flask and part of a primus stove. The search went on for days, and drew a complete blank. Nona was sick with anxiety for Vincent and pleaded with Lao Lee to return to Sungei Riau. At last, in disappointment, the commander gave the order to return to base.

On the way back Nona had a sudden attack of malaria. Fortunately it was not too severe and passed quickly, but it left her weaker than ever and she had to be helped over the more difficult stretches of the route. On reaching the camp Nona discovered to her horror that Vincent had had a very bad attack of fever while she was away, and was now desperately ill. Weakly, he told her that the camp had been under a continual state of tension, with two full-scale alerts following rumours of an impending Japanese attack.

The Japanese were stepping up their anti-guerrilla operations throughout the province, and refugees were pouring into the camps as the enemy carried out severe reprisals against villages suspected of helping the communists. There were horrifying stories of hundreds of civilians being forced to dig their own graves before being machine-gunned.

Because of the danger of attack Lao Lee had all the women and children in the communist camp evacuated to a safer location in the jungle, but they returned later when the immediate danger of a Japanese assault was thought to be over. In July 1944, however, the Japanese launched a major offensive against the guerrilla hideouts, and the non-combatants were once more forced to leave. On her way up the jungle trail with the column of terrified people, Nona could hear the sound of shooting close at hand, and on one occasion they were forced to hide in the undergrowth, holding their breath, while a Japanese patrol passed along a track just below them. There were numerous children in the Malayan column, as well as livestock, and it was impossible to keep them quiet; fortunately the Japanese were making so much noise themselves that they heard nothing and went on their way.

In August 1944 the Japanese struck at the guerrilla hideouts again, this time supported by mortars, but they failed to locate the main headquarters. Nevertheless there was no doubt that the Japanese net was closing in, and Vincent and Nona became more dubious about their chances of survival. Despite their general exhaustion and poor state of health the Europeans were forced to carry out a variety of strenuous tasks, including tree-felling and digging, and now, to make matters worse, they were subjected to daily tirades of venom from a newly arrived Chinese commissar named Lao Fong, who hated the British. He ordered everyone else in the camp to shun them, which came as a bitter blow; up to now they had received nothing but friendliness and respect.

Both Vincent and Nona were now suffering more frequent attacks of malaria, and before long Vincent also developed beri-beri. At the height of their misery, in February 1944, the Japanese launched their biggest attack so far, sweeping deep into the jungle from all sides. No one knew where the Japanese would strike next; camp after camp was attacked and its occupants were slaughtered, each infantry assault being preceded by air strikes.

Before long whole areas of Pahang Province were in flames, and as one plantation after another went up in smoke long columns of refugees – Vincent and Nona among them – moved off to try and find safety deeper in the jungle. The journey was a nightmare. Torn as they were by dysentery they were completely unable to keep down any food, and they were now so weak that they had to be continually supported.

By this time Japanese activity in the jungle was so intense that it was too dangerous for refugees to move in large groups, and the party accompanying the British couple gradually split up. Occasionally gunfire and the crash of grenades reverberated through the trees as armed guerrillas tangled with enemy patrols. Finally, because neither Nona nor Vincent was able to walk any further, their Chinese helpers built a small hut for them on a hillside and left them there, promising to return with food at regular intervals.

Water poured down on them continually and they were unable to light any fires. Nona's leg, which had become infected as the result of a bite, grew steadily worse, and she could only shuffle round painfully on her posterior. Before long the leg was one long, suppurating sore from knee to ankle, and one morning when she woke from a fitful sleep she found to her horror and disgust that it was crawling with maggots. Then she realized that the maggots were eating the pus and cleansing the wound, and left them alone. Finally the maggots disappeared, and it was apparent that the wound was beginning to heal.

Hunger was now the biggest threat, for the Chinese who had been bringing them food fell ill and his visits became fewer. Their water supply had also run out and every day Nona was forced to make an agonizing journey to a water-hole some distance away, dragging herself slowly along. By this time Vincent was so weak that he was unable to move. One morning he asked Nona to light a fire, as he was shivering with cold. With only one match left, and that sodden, she had to refuse. She lay down beside him and tried to warm his trembling body, which was wrapped in a sodden blanket. Suddenly the shivering stopped and he began to twitch violently, kicking out several times. Then he lapsed into a coma.

Frantically she massaged his hands, trying to instil some warmth into his body. At last she decided to risk lighting a fire. She managed to light her solitary match and soon a cheerful flame was flickering among some dry sticks. Then she set about massaging Vincent's limbs once more. It was a long time before she realized that he was beyond all help.

She dragged herself away from the body and lay on the other side of the hut, gripped by a terrible feeling of apathy and despair. Much later four Chinese arrived, and she watched dumbly as they dug a grave and laid the emaciated corpse of her brother to rest, hardly comprehending what had happened.

They laid her on a blanket and took her with them down the winding jungle trail. They built a new shelter for her and left her in the care of a Chinese named Ah Bun. For days on end she lay there listlessly, wanting nothing except to die and find escape from her overwhelming misery. Although her leg was beginning to heal she was still plagued by acute dysentery, and most of her days were spent in dragging herself from the hut into the undergrowth. During this period, when she wept continually until she had no tears left, the little Chinese was kindness itself, bringing her water to cleanse herself and taking away her filthy clothes to wash. He scoured the area for food, scratching in the soil of a nearby devastated plantation for sweet potatoes and catching tiny fish which he roasted. He also gave her his own meagre rice ration, a great act of self-sacrifice for a man who was himself close to starvation.

After some time Nona was once again transferred to another guerrilla camp in the jungle. She developed beri-beri, which the Chinese cured by feeding her a nauseating peanut mash. After that she once more began to grow stronger, although the beri-beri was replaced by huge boils that covered her back, groin and stomach and made it impossible for her to lie in comfort. Many of the guerrillas were also suffering from jungle diseases and some were terribly sick, yet none complained and she was glad to follow their example.

They moved again, this time to a new headquarters that replaced the old one, destroyed by the Japanese. As soon as she was strong enough Nona occupied herself by editing an anti-Japanese newspaper, which gave her a new interest in life. The first edition was distributed in January 1945.

During this period the guerrillas were in communication with members of Force 136, the Allied special duties unit whose agents were parachuted into various parts of Malaya. From this source Nona kept up to date with the war news, which was heartening. In Europe the Germans were on their last legs, and in the Far East the Japanese were gradually being forced out of the territories they had occupied with such lightning speed four years earlier. Such tidings helped to dispel the loneliness she had felt in the months since Vincent's death, but she was never able to feel complete affinity with the Chinese and it was inevitable that she should experience lengthy spells of depression.

She was forced, too, to witness occasional horrifying incidents, such as when four old men, who had been accused of collaborating with the Japanese, were tortured and executed. Everyone in the camp was compelled to watch while guerrillas placed red-hot coals on the backs and feet of the men, and pushed bamboo slivers up their fingernails. The nightmare went on for hours before a party of soldiers dragged the men away and bayoneted them.

In June 1945 there was great excitement in the camp when news arrived that Germany had been defeated. Nona worked non-stop to produce a special edition of her newspaper; it was ready by the following day and on its way for distribution throughout the province.

Japanese attacks on the guerrilla camps continued, but they were weaker now and the enemy patrols consisted mainly of renegade Malay police or Indian troops. Many of the latter in fact deserted to the communists, but they received poor treatment and were consequently resentful.

Gradually Nona became aware of a new and alarming trend. On her travels around the camp she often overheard communist officers holding conversations that boded ill for the future of Malaya once the war was over. Since she had become part of the camp's everyday life they took no notice when she came within earshot, and she heard them talk about the time to come when a general communist offensive would be launched against the authorities if the latter failed to give the Reds a large share in the government of Malaya.

Along with these snatches of conversation came the fear that the communists would hold her as a hostage, and it was with a great sense of relief that, shortly after the end of the war with Japan in September, she read a letter handed to her by a Chinese officer. It was from a Colonel Spencer-Chapman, commanding a Force 136 unit in Kuantan, who invited her to stay with him until arrangements could be made for her transfer to Britain. She could hardly believe her good fortune when the Chinese agreed that she should go to Kuantan the following morning.

So it was that Nona Baker, emaciated and worn after her enforced stay in the jungle, stood on the British parade square at Kuantan with tears streaming down her face, unable to take her eyes from the Union Jack that streamed proudly from the flagpole. A few days later she experienced her supreme triumph when she sat beside British officers on a dais and watched the Japanese troops who had dominated the area for so long throw their weapons into a pile and sullenly give their formal surrender. Incredibly, they were the first Japanese soldiers she had seen.

When she left Kuantan on the first stage of her journey home one of those who came to see her off was Lao Lee, the communist leader whose kindness towards her and her brother had been unstinting. It was the last time she saw him. A long time later she learned that he had been killed by Malayan security forces.

For Nona Baker the ordeal was over; but for Malaya, it was only just beginning.

Bibliography

Braddon, Russell, *Nancy Wake* (London 1956)

Duncan, Sylvia and Peter, *Anne Brusselmans* MBE (London 1959)

Jackson, Robert, *The Red Falcons: The Soviet Air Force in Action* (London 1970)

Marsden, Alexandrina, *Resistance Nurse* (London 1961)

Masters, Anthony, *The Summer that Bled – the Biography of Hannah Senesh* (London 1972)

Reitsch, Hanna, *The Sky my Kingdom* (London 1955)

Smyth, Brigadier Sir John, VC, *The Story of the George Cross* (London 1968)

Suhl, Yuri, *They Fought Back – the Story of Jewish Resistance in Nazi Europe* (London 1968)

Thatcher, Dorothy, and Cross, Robert, *Pai Naa – the Story of Nona Baker* MBE (London 1959)

Tickell, Jerrard, *Odette* (London 1949)

Turner, John Frayn, *A Girl Called Johnnie* (London 1963)